VODKA ON ICE

By the same author

An Alien in Antarctica, McDonald & Woodward, 1997

Forty Years on Ice, The Book Guild, 1998

Foothold on Antarctica, The Book Guild, 1999

VODKA ON ICE

A Year with the Russians in Antarctica

Charles Swithinbank

The Book Guild Ltd
Sussex, England

First published in Great Britain in 2002 by
The Book Guild Ltd
25 High Street,
Lewes, East Sussex
BN7 2LU

Typesetting in Times by
Keyboard Services, Luton, Bedfordshire

Origination, printing and binding in Singapore
under the supervision of MRM Graphics Ltd, Winslow, Bucks

A catalogue record for this book is available from
The British Library

ISBN 1 85776 646 6

The Cold War was in full swing when I joined the Soviet Antarctic Expedition in 1963. By the time I returned home in 1965, I spoke quite fluent Russian and had learned many things that were hardly known west of the Iron Curtain. As the first, and to this day the only Briton to have served with the Soviets in Antarctica, I sought to break down the barriers that, for generations, have separated our cultures.

I dedicate this story to my comrades, with deep respect and gratitude for all that they shared with me.

Charles Swithinbank

CONTENTS

ACKNOWLEDGEMENTS

I am particularly grateful to colleagues who read and commented on the whole or parts of the manuscript: Geoffrey Hattersley-Smith, Bob Headland, Larry Rockhill, Isabella Warren and Bob Wells. Elena Khlinovskaya Rockhill kindly provided insights into life in the USSR. For photographs and permission to use them I thank Norsk Polarinstitutt (pp. 68, 121) and the Arctic and Antarctic Research Institute (p. 76). No family could have been more supportive than my wife Mary, together with Anne, Carol and Kelvin. To them I owe a boundless debt of gratitude.

Charles Swithinbank
Cambridge
April 2001

PROLOGUE

There were icebergs off our starboard side. Far away on the port side I could see pack ice. Beyond that there were gleaming white cliffs—the seaward face of an ice shelf. The good ship *Ob*, named after the great Siberian river, was carrying members of the Soviet Antarctic Expedition. Of the 225 souls on board, I was the only one whose home lay west of the Iron Curtain.

The navigator's chart showed that we were at latitude 69° south, longitude 16° east, a point of some significance in Russia's proud maritime history. It was from this spot or near it that on 17 February 1820 Captain Fabian von Bellingshausen[1] of the Imperial Russian Navy saw the land that we now call Antarctica. It was his second landfall, the first having been farther west.

Was Bellingshausen the discoverer of Antarctica? Probably not. Nobody has ever discovered a continent, and he did not claim to have done so. Indeed, it took landfalls in many places before the concept of an Antarctic continent took shape. Sealing ships operating out of the South Shetland Islands were probably the first to sight parts of the coast. However, Bellingshausen and his men were the first to record seeing a coast backed by the inland ice sheet and ice-covered mountains.

Bellingshausen's expedition had been despatched on the orders of His Imperial Majesty Tsar Alexander I to explore high southern latitudes, higher—if possible—than those reached by Captain James Cook of the Royal Navy during his 1773–1775 circumnavigation in HMS *Resolution*.[2]

Bellingshausen was a Baltic baron, born in 1778 on an island off the coast of Estonia. He had left Kronshtadt in the Gulf of Finland on 26 July 1819 with two ships and 190 men. *Vostok*, a 40-metre armed sloop, was under the command of Captain-Lieutenant Ivan Zavodovskiy, while the smaller 37-metre frigate *Mirny* was under the command of Lieutenant Mikhail Lazarev.

Taking enormous risks with icebergs, pack ice, storms, onshore

1

winds and leaking hulls, the two ships eventually circumnavigated Antarctica before returning to their home port on 24 July 1821.

Bellingshausen's narrative for 17–18 February 1820 describes what he saw. The edge of the ice, he wrote,

> was perpendicular and formed into little coves, whilst the surface sloped upwards towards the south to a distance so far that its end was out of sight even from the mast-head. ... In the farther distance we saw ice-covered mountains...[3]

He was looking at an ice shelf which later came to be named for his second-in-command Captain Lazarev; and beyond it the rising surface of the inland ice sheet.

Captain Fabian von Bellingshausen (1779–1852) of the Imperial Russian Navy

That discovery was 144 years before we of the Ninth Soviet Antarctic Expedition[4] came to ply the same waters. If not for misty weather, we would have been staring in wonder at the very same scene, now from the deck of a ship 50 times the size of *Vostok*. In the far distance we would have seen mountains that could very well be described as ice-covered. As it happened, we had to wait some days to see that far inland.

Lunch that day—16 March 1964—consisted of a bowl of *borsch* with a slice of bread, followed by *compote*—an insipid rust-coloured liquid with a faint taste of boiled apples. I would have to get used to it because I was here of my own free will and it would be 14 months before I would again see my home, family, or familiar food.

Years of often frustrating negotiations had led me to this moment. For the record, I have covered that part of the story in an appendix at the end of this book.

Now, however, I was in the Antarctic and knew that the effort had been worthwhile.

1

Estonia

On 19 October 1963 I opened a telegram at my home in Cambridge instructing me to meet the Soviet liner *Estonia* in the French port of Le Havre on 7 December. Five years had elapsed since I first began working to this end. Although many communications had bypassed me, my file then held 82 letters and 11 telegrams.

I was to be an 'exchange scientist', also the first-ever British member of any Soviet expedition to either the Arctic or the Antarctic. Britain's own permanent Antarctic expedition, the British Antarctic Survey, had agreed to take Dr Garik Grikurov, a Soviet geologist, to Stonington Island, one of their research outposts on the Antarctic Peninsula. I had never met Grikurov and two years were to pass before I had the opportunity of doing so.

I was not new to the business of exploration, having spent two years in the Antarctic with an international expedition[1] and three summer field seasons with American expeditions.[2] But to me, no voyage to the Antarctic will ever be routine. The country is so vast, its nature so varied, its moods so many, and its tiny population so interesting, that one is forever discovering new things.

Although in an average winter the total population of Antarctica then numbered only about 800 men, they came from more than a dozen different nations and formed one of the best examples of internationalism, in word and deed, that could be found at the time. It was in this light that I viewed my participation in the Soviet expedition, and although I had qualms about my own suitability as sole representative of Britain, I had no qualms about the ability of the Russians to look after me and to deliver me safely home at the end of the year.

On this occasion, the decision to leave my wife and children for 18 months was the most painful I have ever made. If they had not accepted the challenge, I would never have agreed to go. When I left home, we shed tears but we knew that the pain was worthwhile.

After a night in Le Havre, I took a taxi to the docks at the appointed hour. A spotlight was trained on the hammer and sickle on a single funnel. It was dusk and *Estonia* was ablaze with lights. The ship was painted white all over and looked very clean. I was apprehensive. Though I had learned about 500 words of Russian, I had never conversed in the language; and I had been told to expect that very few Russians could speak English. Dragging my luggage to the top of the gangway, I took a deep breath.

It was a relief that the first person who spoke to me was a man I knew—Professor Piotr Shumsky. Shumsky was coming south for the Antarctic summer season in company with five French glaciologists.

I was led to a twin-berth cabin and introduced to a handsome young seismologist who spoke quite good English and said that his name was Anatoly Yustinevich Norman. He was 26 years of age, tall, fair, strongly built and, like his surname, Scandinavian in appearance. His home was in Tallinn, Estonia. Knowing that Russians generally address people using their first name together with their middle name (patronymic), I explained that, at that stage at least, I would find 'Anatoly Yustinevich' a bit of a mouthful. I was relieved when he said, 'Just call me Tolya.' I responded, 'I'm Charles.'

I knew that the Russians had a great deal of experience of living in the Arctic, but they had first wintered in the Antarctic only in 1956. Since then they had done their best to make up for lost time. Their permanent stations housed a total of 150 men. Compared with the other ten countries, including the United Kingdom, which maintained stations in the Antarctic, the scale of Soviet work was second only to that of the United States.

There were four Soviet research stations:

	Latitude	Longitude
Mirny	66°33' south	93°01' east
Molodezhnaya	67°40' south	45°51' east
Novolazarevskaya	70°46' south	11°50' east
Vostok	78°27' south	106°52' east

I was to spend a year at Novolazarevskaya with 12 Russians and one Czech. Tolya was the only one who spoke any English. As far as I was concerned, that was ideal, because I planned to speak Russian; yet, whenever I was stumped, I could turn to Tolya. He quickly answered my first pent-up volley of questions about the ship's plans and the expedition's aims, neither of which I had been able to extract from any correspondence with officialdom.

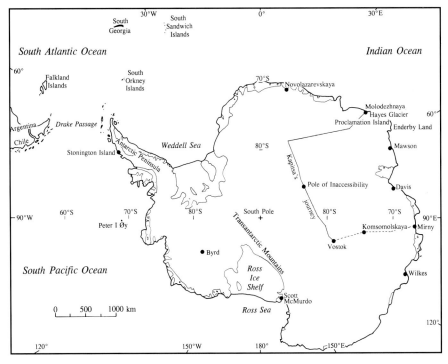

Selected stations in Antarctica (1964) and the route of Kapitsa's journey

Tolya explained that *Estonia* had left the port of Leningrad (now St Petersburg) four days before. We were to sail to Australia via the Suez Canal, and thence to Mirny, the main Soviet research station. After some weeks at Mirny, we would join a bigger ship, *Ob*, and voyage westwards round the coast to our wintering station.

The research activities of the Soviet expedition fell into two groups. First, there were studies of the type normally made at geophysical observatories in other parts of the world: seismology, geomagnetism, earth currents, aurora, cosmic rays, radio propagation, aerology and meteorology. The second category was exploratory: mapping, oceanography, geology, and glaciology—my own subject.

Estonia was not what I expected to find as an expedition ship. Built three years earlier, she was a comfortable passenger liner of 4722 tons,[3] about the size of a cross-channel steamer at the time. Plying between Leningrad, Stockholm, London and Le Havre in the summer months, she was available to go elsewhere during the northern winter. December being summer in the southern hemisphere, she could be used to handle part of the annual staff change-over at the

7

Soviet Antarctic stations. Designed for the Baltic trade, she was ice-strengthened—an essential requirement for penetrating pack ice.

Tolya explained that in a socialist economy, all ships are owned by the state, so it is easy to make full use of one's shipping resources. In jest he asked, 'Why does not the British Antarctic Survey employ the *Queen Mary*, at off-season rates of course, to take their expeditions to the Antarctic?'

In the Soviet Union, he said, the cost of using a ship in the Antarctic was covered by a simple paper transaction. I got the impression that Tolya believed that in the West, ship charter was accomplished by driving to the shipowner's office with bags of gold.

Whether for cash or credit, *Estonia* was not cheap to charter. The expedition was paying 4300 roubles (£1700) per day for her three-month voyage to the Antarctic.

The French party was led by Professor Albert Bauer and belonged to the government-funded Expéditions Polaires Françaises. They would be involved in measuring the rate of movement of the ice sheet along a tractor route directed inland from the coast. Bauer had brought some champagne, and invited a phalanx of local dignitaries and senior Russians to a party in the Customs shed. I was counted in and stood quaffing champagne through formal speeches in French, Russian and English. One of the speeches was by Pavel Senko, the 47-year-old overall leader of the wintering party. He warmly welcomed me and the Frenchmen as a tangible manifestation of their desire for international collaboration.

Back on board I was led into a palatial room which, in passenger service, was the First Class dining-room. There I was introduced to Senko. A small dark wisp of a man, he looked more like a suburban tailor than an expedition leader. Years afterwards I learned that he may have been the first man ever to stand at the North Pole.[4]

Senko was seated at a table for four. Next to him was Dmitry Maksutov, the expedition's chief engineer (who spoke English) and the expedition purser. Maksutov, 40, was tall and fair, and wore glasses. A naval architect by training, he had lived in Flushing, Holland, with his family as 'owner's representative' during the building and fitting out of *Ob*. When his eyes were not focused on anything, they oscillated from side to side, which was disconcerting for me and no doubt for him too.

Senko's opening gesture was to reach for the small and solitary paper napkin on the table. Looking solemn, as if he were about to offer the sacrament, he tore the napkin into four pieces and handed one to each of us. Looking back on it, that act, so small in itself, became to me symbolic of the new world that I had entered. Although

I was full of admiration for many things that the Russians had achieved in 50 years of Soviet rule, it is nevertheless the small things that stick in the mind. If there had been no paper napkin, I should never have realized that they were in short supply.

The meal began with cabbage soup, which I was to come to know quite well, continued with a small plate of *ragu* (ragout), which I was to come to know too well, and ended with *compote*.

Afterwards in the lounge, I was surprised and delighted to meet Sveneld Yevteyev and his wife. Four years earlier, while working with the Americans in Antarctica, Sven and I had lived in a tent together at Cape Crozier, the place whose winter weather was so vividly described by Apsley Cherry-Garrard in *The worst journey in the world*.[5] Sven had then just arrived at the biggest American research station on his first trip abroad. Now that the tables were turned, he said, 'You could not possibly be feeling more bewildered than I was on being introduced to the American way of doing things.' I took his point. Sven now worked for UNESCO in Paris, and had come on board to bid us *bon voyage*.

That night I lay awake wondering at the long train of events that had led me to join this expedition, and the purpose of it all. Why had I chosen to launch myself into a culture that saw itself as being fundamentally opposed—at least in a political sense—to my own? Surely, friends asked, it was a daunting prospect? The Cold War dragged on and the Iron Curtain had an impact on everyone's lives.

For 14 years I had been professionally engaged in glaciology, the study of glaciers and all other forms of ice. I had become interested in how glaciers form and how they move, how and why they have grown in some periods of history and shrunk in others. Glaciology had always been a cosmopolitan branch of science with participants from many countries. Although, when I first lived and worked in Antarctica (from 1950 to 1952), we were almost alone on the continent, only five years later ten different expeditions were there and each was involved, among other things, with glaciology.

In keeping up with my subject I had read most of the publications resulting from this work. However, there was one big gap. The Russians, who were doing more glaciological work than any of the smaller countries, were publishing in Russian. I could not blame them for that—but neither could I read them.

One solution would have been for some institution to translate all their literature into English, but that was impracticable. The alternative was to learn Russian. However, a friend had spent 18 months studying it full-time, so I had no illusions about polishing off the task at evening classes. The easiest way would be to combine what had become my normal work in the Antarctic with 18 months of living the new language.

At the same time I had some curiosity about the theory and practice of socialism, although my own political views had never been left of centre. Marx and Lenin, I had read, believed that socialism was only a stepping stone towards their Elysian vision of true communism. How far, I wondered, had their ideas progressed? For example, how had it come about that in less than half a century, followers of this new ideology had grown to outnumber the followers of some of the world's great religions? With more than a billion believers—or so we were told—was communism the wave of the future?

These and other questions troubled me. How was it that, from 1942 to 1945, an initially ill-equipped Soviet army halted superior German forces at the gates of Moscow, at the gates of Leningrad, and in the streets of Stalingrad—before driving them back to the very heart of Germany? Did politics have something to do with it?

How was it that the Soviet Union had bested the supposed technological superiority of the United States by lofting the first Earth satellite; had put the first man into orbit around the Earth; and had kept its people fed, housed and happy while all the time avoiding the scourge of unemployment? Did politics have anything to do with it?

While aware of their successes, I knew that Stalin had consigned more of his own countrymen to the grave in peacetime than had Hitler's armies in war; that there were more KGB agents and informants monitoring Soviet citizens at home than there were Soviet spies operating abroad; that Russia's so-called 'wars of national liberation' were in reality wars for the suppression of political opposition; that the 'democratic republics' of eastern Europe were anything but democratic; that Russian dissidents were sent to Siberia, exiled abroad, or incarcerated in psychiatric hospitals; that the press was tightly controlled by the state and that an 'exit' visa was harder to obtain that an entry visa to a foreign country.

It was like the riddle of the sphinx. Would I have any answers 18 months from now?

On rising the next morning, I followed Tolya into the dining-room. There, Shumsky beckoned me to join him and Bauer at a small table, and there we stayed at mealtimes for the rest of the voyage. We were waited on by a strongly built but very friendly girl named Zoya Pavlova. Zoya had wide-set, faintly Mongolian eyes, dark hair and a constant cheerful smile.

I would have preferred to get to know my comrades-to-be, but Shumsky wanted the small contingent of foreigners to be immersed in his culture by stages. Shumsky himself was a stocky, genial academic, well-known in the West through his devotion to scholarship and his disdain for politics. He spoke five languages fluently. His textbook *Principles of Structural Glaciology* commanded so much respect that it was translated and published in English at the expense of the US Government.[6]

After breakfast consisting of porridge, bread, butter and jam, with unlimited coffee, the expedition personnel—though not the ship's crew—were allowed ashore in Le Havre. It was decreed that they must walk in threes, and that at least one of each group must be a full member of the Communist Party. This was to guard against the possibility of defection and also, if necessary, to deal with any untoward incident with the inhabitants. For some of the younger Russians it offered their first steps on foreign soil, so they jumped at the opportunity. None of them was given any French money, so window-shopping was the order of the day. From the array of cameras they could easily have been mistaken for American tourists; in fact the resemblance came in handy at another port. Excitement ran high as they photographed cyclists and pedestrians, cars and shop-windows, bourgeois villas and peasant cottages—and later the photographs were captioned in those terms.

Estonia sailed at 1630.[7] That evening I was invited to a party to meet the other 13 members of the Novolazarevskaya team. In typical Russian fashion, there was lots of vodka to smooth over the language difficulties. The leader was 32-year-old Nikolay Yeremin, a short, athletic pale blond with a bullet-shaped head and a ready smile. I sensed a feeling of relief among the Russians that their anxiously scrutinized representative of the capitalist world, as they saw it, appeared at first sight to be relatively human. '*Na zdorovye!*' (To your health) rang out a good many times that evening.

Fearing that at age 37 I might be older than most, I was happy to discover that the doctor was 43 and the cook was 46. Our average age, it turned out, was 35 years. This was as much as a decade older than the average age of men on British polar expeditions. Of the 14 men, 12 were married and between us we had 19 children. All had previous experience in the Arctic or Antarctic. Later I learned that between the 14 of us we had spent 70 years at work in the Arctic or Antarctic.

This professionalism was in marked contrast with the practice in other countries, where opportunities for permanent employment in polar research were few. British expeditions were staffed by young men who would spend the rest of their lives doing something else. The mature staffing of the Soviet expedition was made possible by having a large organization, the Arctic and Antarctic Research

11

Institute in Leningrad, where more than 2000 men and women found permanent employment, most of them in Arctic work. In Britain, by contrast, there were only a handful of people who had spent more than a few years either directly engaged in polar research or professionally connected with it.

The Russians compensated their men for prolonged absences from home by paying them from two to five times their salary at home, the lower-paid men getting the greater proportional supplement. It was a shock to find that I, who was paid a normal salary for a research worker at a British university, was receiving less than the lowest-paid of my Soviet *tovarishchy* (comrades).[8] However, knowing that in material terms my standard of living at home was much higher than theirs, I shed no tears.

The following day it was arranged that I should submit to a crash course in Russian at the hands of Ayzik Nudelman, formerly a meteorologist but now serving as chronicler and historian of Soviet Antarctic expeditions. He was a short, balding, 46-year-old man with a lazy eye and a biting contempt for my struggles to pronounce Russian sounds. Two one-hour lessons a day left me exhausted, but at the same time with a rapidly expanding vocabulary.

In exchange for my Russian lessons, I was asked to give some English lessons in the expedition leader's air-conditioned suite on the boat deck. Senko, Maksutov, and Nudelman were my pupils. They wanted pronunciation rather than grammar or syntax, and I read to them from books and magazines. Unfortunately, none of them wanted to do any homework. It became clear that, having had access all their lives only to Russian teachers of English, they hoped that the arrival on the scene of an Englishman would act as an elixir leading to a rapid mastery of the language. They improved, but mastery eluded them.

I started to get acquainted with the Frenchmen on board. Albert Bauer, their leader, had a wife and nine children at his home in Strasbourg. He was a short, rotund, jovial 47-year-old who looked more like Humpty Dumpty than anyone I had ever met. He had been on expeditions to Greenland, but this was his first trip to Antarctica. As assistants he brought Jacques Bulle, Pierre Camaret, Pierre Chaveyron and Jean Charpentier. Their objective was to measure the rate of flow and deformation of the ice sheet in central Antarctica, this being one small step in establishing whether or not the amount of ice was increasing under present climatic conditions.[9]

The Frenchmen were noisy, cheerful and friendly. But since they were to return home with the ship at the end of the short Antarctic summer, most of them did not bother to learn Russian. There were occasions on which serious attempts to communicate gave way to wild gesticulations on the French side and bear-like shrugs on the Russian. Yet good humour prevailed on both sides.

It took a week to reach Port Said and the Suez Canal. Some Egyptian traders jumped aboard and others sought to barter from their boats. Their initial enthusiasm vanished when they realized that the Russians had only roubles to offer. Never were so few goods traded aboard such an affluent-looking vessel. The canal itself was busy, though we were able to join a southbound convoy the next day. I came on deck to see what looked like a desert mirage. A mile away, as clear as could be, an oil tanker was gliding silently across the sand dunes. *Estonia* was in the canal so the tanker, it seemed, must be high and dry. Then someone explained that there were two canals at this point; the tanker was in the northbound channel which we could not see. Our progress slowed when a tanker ahead of us ran aground, but *Estonia* was allowed to use the northbound channel to by-pass the obstruction, so there was very little delay.

I learned that our ship had a crew of 93 and that there were 132 expedition members on board, ranging in age from 22 to 51. Most were Russians but, in an ethnic sense, I recognized a number with Armenian, Jewish, Turkic or Mongol features. The Captain was a wiry Armenian by the name of Aron Oganov.

In 1963 the general absence of women in the Antarctic was held to be one of the greatest privations—or one of the greatest blessings—depending on your point of view. On *Estonia*, however, there were 30 women. Most of them were employed in domestic duties, though a few were officers in the purser's or catering staff. The Purser's assistant was Zhenya Sharova, a petite, shy brunette who spoke fluent English. On the Baltic passenger runs, Zhenya was the buffer between the English-speaking passengers and the ship's staff.

A couple of lusty carpenters had constructed a sizeable swimming pool two metres deep on the after cargo hatch. Bathing was mixed, and the pool was in use day and night. On sunny days the upper deck was sometimes strewn with women in the briefest forms of attire. Though not unwelcome, this was for me an unfamiliar aspect of life on an Antarctic expedition. At the time, no British or American polar ships carried women.

Evenings were spent watching films, none of them remarkable but all entertaining. After working hours, there were no rules nor even etiquette requiring the crew to keep separate from the passengers. As if by magic, blue jeans and drab domestic uniforms gave way to summer frocks and cocktail dresses. Several women who, in their working clothes, had been virtually indistinguishable from the male members of the crew, now drew admiring glances. There was music and dancing under soft lights and, as the evening drew on, couples would wander on deck and lean on the guard rail. By moonlight the scene could be mistaken for life on an ocean liner.

As we passed through the Red Sea, the dances moved on deck. I noticed liaisons progressing from a stolen kiss in a dark corner to more intimate encounters behind locked doors. Although these affairs became public knowledge, fraternizing was considered a private matter and of no concern to others.

In taking photographs of my companions, I noticed that, as soon as a camera was pointed in their direction, all traces of a smile vanished from their faces. It was not that they objected to being photographed— it was simply the custom to look serious. They proudly showed me photographs of their families and there too there were no smiles. The expressions reminded me of studio daguerreotype photographs from the days of my grandfather.

How could I take home such a depressing record of the Russians I had worked with? Who would believe me when I claimed that, off-camera, they smiled as readily as my own countrymen? I hurried to the dictionary and extracted the word for smile. '*Ulybayetes*!' I exclaimed, and they smiled. '*Ulybayetes*' it was for every photograph from then on.

Estonia glided into Aden harbour early on 21 December. The only passengers allowed ashore were Shumsky, the French group, and me. Whereas most of the Russians knew—like soldiers—that management decisions were not to be questioned, Senko the expedition leader had realised that passengers from the Western world would be up in arms if confined to the ship for no good reason.

Assuming from the language of our conversation that we were all French, our taxi driver launched into a tirade on the shortcomings of the British administration. The Frenchmen could scarcely contain their laughter and provoked him to further rantings to embarrass me. Anxious to conceal my identity at a time when hand grenades were being used on the streets, I readily agreed about *La perfide Albion*. Shumsky thought the incident so funny that later, much to my discomfort, he told half the expedition about it.

Relishing the temporary freedom ashore, Shumsky had bought a short-wave radio to hear foreign broadcast stations, although he knew that such things were frowned upon in Russia. I received mail on board and was able to send some from the harbour post office.

2

Beyond Australia

From Aden we set course for Fremantle, the port of Perth in western Australia; it was to be our last call before heading south for Antarctica. As we approached the Equator on Christmas Eve, a contest was held on deck between two of the main expedition groups, the 'Geophysical' and the 'Aeromet'. The contest involved oratory, poetry, instrumental music, dancing, pageantry and seamanship, all entered into with gusto, with some very ingenious fancy dress. Although a lot of it passed over my head, it did show me that Russians, like the rest of us, could let their hair down. One act consisted of an appropriately dressed pair doing the twist to the sound of an American dance record. Though not approved by the Ministry of Culture at home, it was considered an acceptable extravagance in the Indian Ocean. Senko, Shumsky, the Captain, and the Chief Pilot B.A. Minkov were the judges. Aeromet won by a narrow margin.

Shumsky generously arranged for Bauer and me to be supplied with liquor from the ship's store to celebrate Christmas, a feast that was not celebrated by anyone else—at least not in public. I got two bottles of Georgian *champanskoe* (champagne) and a case of Czech beer. The French were given 'cognac'. Curiously enough, none of the Russians knew that champagne was named after a district in France. One Russian explained that *cognac* was a well-known product of Georgia. With raised eyebrows the Frenchmen drank it—and enjoyed it.

I invited the Novolazarevskaya crew to a party. They came to the cabin in procession, the leader holding a lighted candle on a fir twig, with the gift of a picture book of Leningrad signed by all my colleagues. It was the first of many touching gestures that spoke of their yearning for friendship with anyone from outside their realm. It was a peace offering from the heart.

Some hours later I invited the Frenchmen for a Christmas party. They arrived with a bottle of cognac for me to drink during the winter, and in return I offered them some whisky that I had brought from home. I had also brought with me a tape-recorder, and now my guests

15

were able to relax as I played the annual Christmas carol service sung in the chapel of King's College, Cambridge. Thinking of home, I had tears in my eyes and so did some of the Frenchmen.

Estonia crossed the Equator during the night after Christmas. For a week I had been puzzled by the sight of some of the girls spending their evenings sitting on deck picking oakum—laboriously separating the strands of old rope. In days of old this was a task reserved for convicts and paupers, but our girls were neither and they seemed to enjoy it. The real purpose only became clear when King Neptune and his Queen, in most elaborate costumes, marched on deck followed by many attendants. The King was disguised behind a metre-long white beard and silver crown. Many of his staff were clad only in 'grass' skirts made from the old rope. I had seen many crossing-the-line ceremonies in which, as a poor substitute, some of the men were dressed and padded in the appropriate places to represent women. But here I was witnessing a much more attractive proposition. After many speeches and much cheering, a gang of wild, half-naked and painted 'devils' appeared and, with blood-curdling yells, set about heaving people into the swimming pool. I was captured by one of the devils and dropped unceremoniously on top of others. Even two women who could not swim were pushed head-over-heels into the mêlée before being dragged—terrified—to safety. Apart from these two, much fun was had by all.

In the evening we were summoned to the lounge, where the Captain handed out crossing-the-line certificates. A glass of wine and an orange were offered to each of us, after which we were led onto the promenade deck where, under a starry sky, dancing and carousing continued into the small hours. The Captain danced with the lowliest of stewardesses, reminding them that—within limits—they belonged to a supposedly classless society. Off-duty moments like these could be delightfully informal, though at other times I noted a clear-cut deference to rank, surely a feature of the Soviet system itself.

Apart from feast days, the food was not good. There was always plenty of it, but there were fewer high-protein foods than in a typical Western diet. The meat in particular was of poor quality, with an excess of gristle and bone. I spent the next 15 months wondering where the good meat was consumed in the Soviet Union. Politics being a preoccupation of Man rather than animals, I saw no reason why communist beef should be less tender than capitalist beef. Somebody *must* be getting the good meat. It was not until two years later, in talking to a woman who had lived in the Soviet Union, that I was disillusioned. She said that artificial cattle foods designed to produce tender beef, although quite general in the West, were

16

unknown in the Soviet Union. Soviet cattle have to eat what they can get.

Cabbage soup was served at least once a day. It was of two kinds, *borsch* and *shchi*, which use different varieties of cabbage, though the principal ingredient was always potatoes. There was black bread and white bread, both of them freshly baked. The butter was delicious and never in short supply. One of the most pleasing compensations for the heat of the tropics was that, whenever the air temperature rose above a certain point, there was a general issue of white wine at the rate of half a bottle per person per day.

At this stage of the voyage, *Estonia* was maintaining a speed of almost 17 knots in calm water, putting $3\frac{1}{2}$ degrees of latitude behind her every day. Twice daily, as a schoolboy in awe of his teacher, I submitted to Comrade Nudelman's Russian lessons. I could tell by the pained expression on his face that my pronunciation was still considered pathetic. In an attempt to see what he was driving at, I tape-recorded both his words and my attempts to imitate them. Listening alone to the tape later, I could not tell the difference. But he persisted and I persisted. Gradually I was beginning to understand what people were saying to me.

Shumsky asked me to translate his latest research paper into English as he wished to submit it to the *Journal of Glaciology*. I gasped at the thought of translating highly technical Russian within weeks of beginning to learn the language but, with the help of my teacher and a dictionary, the job was done.

New Year celebrations included a concert, singing and dancing. I was invited by Senko to a small table with Maksutov and Shumsky. A tumbler of cognac was placed before each of us. Then began a whole series of toasts—to peace, to friendship, to wives and sweethearts, to the success of our expedition and to many other things. Just as our glasses were being refilled, my peripheral vision became obscured and I felt that perhaps I was having a stroke. Holding firmly on to the table, I sat down and realized what is meant by the words 'blind drunk'. Later, I recalled that we had not eaten for seven hours—hence my problem.

The ensuing feast included caviar (black and red), pickled herring, pickled fungus, sausage, crabmeat, tomatoes, and fruit. One after another, toasts were drunk to *Mir i druzhba* (peace and friendship), sentiments that not everyone believed were shared by people in the West.

We arrived off Fremantle on 3 January 1964. After being inspected for infectious diseases, the ship was allowed alongside, at which point we were invaded by newspaper and television reporters. The arrival

Concert audience on *Estonia*

of a Soviet passenger liner was rare and thus of much interest. I was asked whether I had been brainwashed and the Frenchmen were asked if they were communists. Some Russian émigrés brought their wives and children on board to talk to the crew. While most were satisfied with their lives in Australia, they were at the same time nostalgic for news of the old country.

In contrast to Aden, here in Australia everyone was allowed ashore but, as in France, only in groups of three. One man told me that one of his reasons for volunteering for Antarctic work was that it was the only practicable way for him to see a little of foreign countries. The Russians were each given £10 for spending money—not much considering that, to them, the shops were filled with unimagined luxuries.

Having nothing with which to entertain my comrades in Antarctica, I bought a gallon of sherry and three gallons of Australian port. Then the Frenchmen and I hired a car. Unfortunately, the only car available was a rather ostentatious new Plymouth automatic. This attracted great attention when we drew up alongside *Estonia*. The Russians were astonished that hiring a car was possible, and they descended on the scene to photograph the vehicle from every angle. The last thing I wanted was to appear affluent; I felt like sticking a notice on the windscreen to explain that five of us were sharing the cost.

With Shumsky and four of the Frenchmen, I drove on a sightseeing tour inland to the Serpentine dam. There we were amazed to discover that, after less than 50 kilometres (km) of driving through the forested coastal belt, we came to the edge of the great Australian desert.

Back on board, I found incoming mail piled on my bunk. I had already posted my own letters. With the exception of a few enterprising people who bought Australian stamps, the Russians neither received mail nor sent any. Their mail had been sent from Leningrad by diplomatic bag, and it was planned to send mail home the same way. However, the bag was never delivered in Fremantle and the outgoing mail, having Russian stamps on it, could not be posted ashore. Now they had missed the only opportunities since leaving home. It would be another 15 months before they could read a letter from home.

This was the first of a number of incidents that opened my eyes to the extraordinary tolerance of Soviet citizens in the face of bureaucratic bungling. It contrasted with the decidedly intolerant attitude of Soviet authority towards erring individuals. Tolya dismissed the problem with a shrug of the shoulders; like his comrades, he took life as it came. To think how things might have been would serve no purpose.

A small crowd watched as *Estonia* left the dock, and then a few hundred Saturday-night strollers waved from the pierhead. Why, they must have wondered, would anyone want to leave this equable climate to head for isolation in a frozen land?

Two days after leaving Fremantle we entered the roaring forties, that great belt of stormy ocean which, together with the furious fifties and the screaming sixties, circles the globe without encountering any land mass. All who go south must cross it. *Estonia* behaved well in high seas, parting the waves with her prow, rolling gently, and never wallowing or pounding or shuddering as some ships do. Many of the landlubbers failed to appear for meals. Without the supply of seasick pills that I had brought, I too would have been confined to my bunk. *Estonia* maintained at least 15 knots through fair weather and foul.

For the first few days, Australian fruit and vegetables appeared at mealtimes, but soon we were back to *borsch*, *shchi*, and boiled Russian potatoes with small portions of meat or fish.

Estonia was less than four days from the bleaching heat of Fremantle when the sea temperature dropped to 5°C and the ship became enveloped in mist under a leaden sky. The same day we caught sight of the first iceberg. In these latitudes the icebergs had been decimated by melting and were no bigger than houses, but they came from Antarctica, and one could sense the rising level of excite-

19

ment of the men who had not been here before. For me too the first iceberg, and the last one on the way home, will always have an emotional significance.

Our first destination was to be Mirny, the principal Soviet station in Antarctica. Mirny lies almost on the Antarctic Circle (66°32'S) at 93° east of Greenwich—about the same longitude as the Bay of Bengal. The Antarctic Circle is defined as the latitude north of which the sun rises and sets every day of the year, and south of which one can see the midnight sun in summer. Being on the Antarctic Circle, Mirny only saw the midnight sun once a year, on Midsummer Day.

The other Soviet stations were Vostok, 1550 km south of Mirny; Molodezhnaya, 2300 km round the coast to the west; and Novolazarevskaya, 1500 km beyond that. While at Mirny, all expedition members bound for Molodezhnaya or Novolazarevskaya would transfer to the expedition's cargo/passenger ship *Ob* before steaming westwards along the coast.

Although nine other countries occupied bases in the Antarctic, they were well spread. Such is the vastness of this land, that on the main part of the continent south of the Antarctic Circle, the density of population in winter is measured, not as elsewhere in persons per square kilometre, but instead in thousands of square kilometres per person. In round figures there were in 1964 about 18,000 square kilometres available for each of us. Not for us was the problem of where to erect the garden fence; and not—we hoped—for generations to come.

Albert Bauer held a party to celebrate his birthday. Apart from Shumsky, there were no Russians present. Shumsky had always been something of a rebel. He had attended scientific conferences abroad and had a reputation for speaking his mind. That in itself made him an object of interest to the KGB.[1] I noted that he was generally circumspect in the presence of the expedition's management, presumably because one of them must be involved with the KGB. But here in a private cabin he could relax. He told us that he was a member of the Russian Orthodox Church and also of the Communist Party, the first because he was a believer and the second because it was expected of a person in his position. Like Bauer, he was 48 years old and portly.

We knew that Shumsky enjoyed a high reputation among Western scientists and, had he ever chosen to defect, he would have been offered a choice of professorships. He told us that his grandfather was a real Cossack with a handlebar moustache. Shumsky himself had lived in Kharkov in the Ukraine from 1916 to 1932, after which he moved to Leningrad, serving as leader at one of the Franz Josef Land weather stations in 1947–48. Finally he moved to Moscow in 1950.

In discussing his life at home, he confided that it was only four years since he had secured a flat of his own. Before that, like most Russian families, he had had no choice but to share his three rooms with another family.

Looking at newspaper photographs, I remarked to Shumsky that the ideal Russian woman appeared to be plump. 'Only in the country,' he quipped; 'in cities we like them slim.'

The following day I could see about 50 icebergs of all shapes and sizes, weird forms like mountain peaks, a face, a cottage, an island or some sleeping animal. We could also see pack ice, not formidable as it sometimes appears but loose and easily penetrated. The plan was to stop here to await the arrival of *Ob*. Although *Ob* had sailed from Leningrad at the same time as *Estonia*, she had not come via the Suez Canal but instead via the Cape of Good Hope. Unlike *Estonia*, *Ob* was a cargo/passenger ship designed to transit the sea route from the Atlantic to the Pacific along the north coast of Siberia.[2] This meant that she had a skin thick enough to withstand the shock of meeting even heavy ice floes, whereas *Estonia* could only nudge the ice out of her way at slow speed.

Just as *Ob* appeared, a twin-engined aircraft made a low pass over us, wings rocking wildly. It was the traditional airman's greeting. They knew that not only were we carrying parcels and letters from home but also fresh fruit and vegetables for them. We were also carrying next winter's personnel; those who had already wintered could look forward to handing over their duties and departing with the ships when they headed north.

As the two ships approached, sirens sounded, fireworks were launched into the air and everyone on deck waved and cheered. *Ob* led the way southwards and we followed. A convoy maintains the speed of the slowest ship, so we weaved silently and sedately through the night like a puppy at the heels of its master, keeping our station 500 metres astern of *Ob*.

By morning, gazing out across the ever-changing ice fields, we finally felt transported from the world of ordinary mortals to a more splendid place. Emperor penguins porpoised through the water and marched in single file across the floes. Here and there the dorsal fins of killer whales broke surface. Dotted on the ice there were seals looking like so many sacks of coal, and only when we brushed past and shook their floes did they raise an almost snake-like head from one end of the coal sack. They resented our intrusion, and we realized what an oddity the ships must have seemed to them.

On our port beam there rose a dazzling, snow-white island—an ice dome so smooth and symmetrical in outline that it could have been drawn with a compass. It was Drygalski Island, 20 km across and rising to 300 metres above sea level. Fringed on all sides by ice cliffs 30 metres high, it was unscalable from the sea. The Russians considered the island to be such a perfect replica-in-miniature of an ice-covered continent that they had sent people to study it. No rock was visible, and seismic ice-depth sounding had shown that nowhere does the underlying rock basement rise above sea level. It was, in short, an ice-cap built on nothing more than a submarine shoal.

Now there were many more icebergs in sight. The characteristic form of Antarctic icebergs is tabular and, though they may capsize and decay into the irregular forms that we had seen earlier, most of them retain a flat or gently domed upper surface that seldom rises more than 30 metres above sea level. In size they can be colossal. Single icebergs have been reported with dimensions of over 280 km

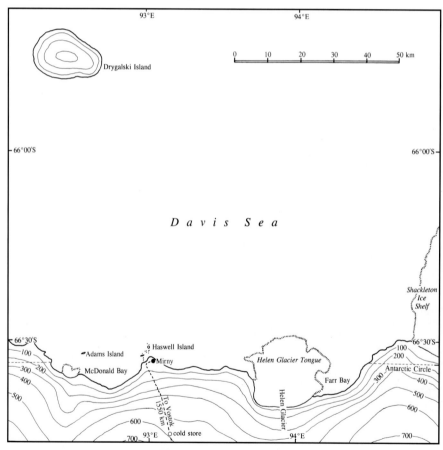

The approaches to Mirny

and areas exceeding 10,000 square kilometres. Those we now saw were nearly all the same size—a kilometre across with a badly crevassed and distinctly dome-shaped surface. Some people have called them 'bread-crust' icebergs, because they look a bit like loaves of bread. Since they were clustered together in groups we guessed that many of them were not moving but instead grounded on shoals.

'Antarctica in sight!' a meteorologist yelled as he passed our cabin. The sun was shining, the sea was calm, and before us lay the great ice sheet, its smooth white surface plunging towards a line of coastal ice cliffs. It was an awe-inspiring sight. There are many kinds of beauty in landscape but there is nothing so clean and so undefiled as an Antarctic landscape. It leaves people breathless with admiration and makes them feel very small.

Having negotiated one hazard—the pack ice—we came to the next, a 30-km-wide belt of fast ice that kept us from reaching Mirny. Fast ice is a continuous unbroken sheet of ice attached to the coast. It forms in winter and most of it breaks up of its own accord to drift to sea in late summer; but it was not yet late summer.

Ob began cutting into ice that was from one to two metres thick. Every time the ship charged, she was forced to a standstill after 100 metres or so. *Estonia* could either wait for *Ob* to break a channel towards the shore, which might take weeks, or we could unload the fresh food supplies and some of the passengers where we were.

The Captain decided to moor to the edge of the fast ice with hawsers stretching to logs—or 'deadmen' as they are known—firmly frozen into the ice. Everyone descended the gangway to stretch their legs. A football appeared, and there followed a wild and enthusiastic game without rules or referee. One little Adélie penguin was so consumed with curiosity that it marched fearlessly into the game, flapping its stubby little wings and squawking whenever one of the players, in brushing too close, seemed not to respect its dignity. Finally it retreated, shaking its head and evidently wondering about the point of it all.

Shumsky used a hand auger to drill through the ice. It was less than one metre thick, but he declared that it was strong enough to support an aircraft. Shortly afterwards the twin-engined machine that flew over us the previous day made a ski-landing beside the ship. Out clambered a string of identically-clad men in leather suits and fur-lined helmets. I witnessed a peculiarly Russian form of greeting as each man fell into the arms of someone from the ship, kissing both cheeks and hugging heartily. As a mark of special friendship, it seemed, men planted kisses on each other's lips. Having never before seen grown males greet each other in this way, I fell to wondering what transcendent form of greet-

A Lisunov-2 landing beside *Estonia*

ing must be in store for the ladies on board. This should be worth watching, so I followed the newcomers. It was a disappointment when I saw one of them shake the hand of a pretty stewardess, while another, more daring, planted a tentative kiss on her cheek. Evidently there was much that I had to learn about etiquette.

The aircraft was a Lisunov-2 (Li-2), equipped with skis in place of wheels and unmistakably a copy of the American Douglas DC-3 (Dakota). When later I remarked on this to the pilot, he said yes; it was built in the Soviet Union in the Second World War under licence from the Douglas company, which had supplied the plans. The arrangement was part of the wartime Lend-Lease programme, so presumably the licence would have been cheap.

After a conference on board, the Li-2 began a shuttle service taking passengers and baggage to Mirny. The shuttle continued all night, with the pilot shutting down his engines immediately on touchdown before coasting silently to a halt. Interrupted by spells of bad weather, the shuttle service was to continue for a week.

A heavy tractor arrived from Mirny hauling a steel cargo-sledge. As the tractor weighed 13 tonnes and the ice was slushy and rotten, I did not envy the driver. When the sledge was loaded and the tractor moved off, a storm blew up, and *Estonia* cast off and put to sea to ride it out.

On 14 January, three smiling ship's officers appeared in my cabin and shook my hand. I was not sure what this signified, until I was given a telegram from my wife announcing the birth of our son. Then I too was smiling. Although the telegram assured me that all was well, I was anxious for some time afterwards. But 15,000 km from home, as we were then, I was powerless to help. Sooner or later, generally as a means of escape from this feeling of utter helplessness about things at home, Antarctic men tend to retreat into a protective shell in which they think as little as possible of what might be going on, or going wrong, in their absence.

The Purser appeared with a bottle of champagne 'from the Captain and crew'. A party ensued at which a dozen people consumed half a gallon of vodka, half a gallon of my Australian port, and a bottle of red wine. I had intended the port to be savoured only during the winter together with my closest friends. However, I was told that, in Russia, any bottle placed on a table must be drained to the last drop, even if some of those consuming it slide under the table before the bottle is empty. I had learned my lesson.

A telegram came from Admiral James R. Reedy, commander of the US Naval Support force in Antarctica, congratulating me on the birth of my son. Evidently news travelled fast, even here.

3

The Pentagon

It was three days before the storm blew itself out. By then the ice we had moored against had drifted out to sea; so the ship moved 80 km along the coast to the east and secured to fast ice at the junction between Shackleton Ice Shelf and the land ice. We had a good view up-slope to a glacier comprising great ice blocks cascading towards the sea and, on its surface, an outcrop of moraine.

Making known that I would like to see something of Mirny, I was woken at 0400 and told that, if I was quick, I could fly ashore with a cargo of fresh vegetables and condensed milk. I threw some clothes into a bag and raced out to find the plane already running up its engines. Jumping aboard, I noted that none of the cargo was lashed

A grey day off the Shackleton Ice Shelf

down. Nobody suggested that I should use a seat-belt: there was none. After take-off I ambled to the cockpit to find that none of the three crew wore a seat-belt. This, I was to learn, was standard practice except in turbulent weather.

We passed Helen Glacier, 17-km wide and pushing an ice tongue 20 km out to sea. The whole coastline seemed more dangerously crevassed than any I had seen before. I spied two tiny rock outcrops immediately behind the coastal ice cliffs. Between the outcrops were black specks of various shapes and sizes—and I realized that these must be Mirny. I was alarmed to note that crevasses surrounded the station, extending on one side to within a stone's throw of the buildings. There were two runways marked out on the ice, and we landed on the shorter one. At one end there was an ice cliff that dropped 20 metres to the sea, and at the other end there were some gaping crevasses.

I helped to unload the cargo and then rode to the station on a sledge behind a tractor, still sitting on our tonne of condensed milk. Led through a door that looked like the entrance to a dungeon, I descended a wooden staircase into the dining-hut for breakfast. As the cooks had to cater for 86 men during the winter and double that number during the annual change-over period, things were a bit crowded, with serried ranks of oilcloth-covered tables and hard wooden benches.

Mirny

27

I found that the food was distinctly better than on *Estonia*. On enquiry it was explained that the messing allowance on an Antarctic station was 85 roubles (£34) per man/month, whereas in the ships it was only 58 roubles (£23). Good food was to be our compensation for the absence of stewardesses. Each man served himself from a row of giant cooking pots.

There was a soda fountain machine in the corner. A pull of a lever gave forth half a mug of soda water, accompanied by loud belching noises. As one of the Frenchmen remarked wistfully as he tapped it, *'Il manque seulement le whisky.'*

I was introduced to Mikhail Somov, the overall—as opposed to wintering—leader of the expedition. A tall man of 56, he greeted me with sparkling eyes and a broad smile, contrasting with the generally guarded introductions I had often encountered. Although he spoke little English, I at once sensed an affinity between us. Somov had flown to Mirny seven weeks earlier with a pair of Ilyushin-18 (Il-18) airliners carrying altogether 83 people. This was their way to ensure that the summer activities got under way long before the ships arrived. The Il-18 is a fast turboprop aircraft without ski-landing gear, so could not land at Mirny until snow had been cleared from the runways to leave a foundation of hard snow-free ice. Instead they landed on a bare-ice airstrip in the Bunger Hills, 350 km to the east of Mirny; from there the passengers were ferried to Mirny in Il-14 and Li-2 skiplanes. As soon as the Mirny runways were clear on 7 December, the Il-18s flew in. Three weeks later they flew to Christchurch, New Zealand, and on homeward.

Somov was an oceanographer of such distinction that, 12 years later, a research vessel the size of *Ob* was named after him. A 4-kopek postage stamp featured his portrait together with the *Mikhail Somov*. He was a Hero of the Soviet Union, holder of the Order of Lenin, and had even been awarded the Patron's Medal of the Royal Geographical Society of London. I found him delightfully approachable, a man of wide interests and bold ideas for promoting research and collaboration in Antarctica.

After breakfast, there was a discussion about what to do with me. Evidently they felt that courtesy required them to provide an escort; yet everyone was extremely busy with the handover from the old to the new crew. I would have been happy to tour the station alone. Their solution was to put me on a sledge-load of vegetables and other perishable foods to be driven to the cold store, a snow cave 23 km inland at a height of 600 metres above sea level. It turned out to be a useful sightseeing tour. The climate of Mirny station at this time of the year was such that thawing temperatures were common, so the

Gable roof under construction at Mirny

only place to keep food frozen was inland. The snow cave was 10 metres deep and very cold.

Back at Mirny, I was now able to wander by myself. Seeing crevasses nearby, I stepped only where there were already footsteps. On the seaward side there was an ice cliff. The station was originally built on rock outcrops or bare ice surfaces that were now hidden under snowdrifts created by the buildings themselves. Most of the buried huts were flat-roofed, and they were being excavated by working parties with shovels. The weight of snow was so great that the roofs had begun to cave in and, as the snow melted, there were floods indoors.

To avert future problems, teams of builders were erecting gable roofs over each flat roof. Sawn timber was expensive or unobtainable, so the joists and rafters were hewn by hand from unbarked Siberian pine logs. The bark was stripped with an adze and joints were fashioned using only an axe. Such skills, I mused, were long since lost in the West. Light planking was laid over the roof and, finally, galvanized steel sheeting.

There were doorways at different levels, each leading to an inside stairway. The highest door was for use in winter when the huts were buried, the lowest for summer, with a halfway door for seasons in between.

29

Tiered entrances to a hut at Mirny

The base leader's hut was known as 'the Pentagon', in reference to that place from which all orders for the conduct of affairs in the United States were believed to emanate. Approaching it, I noted an array of national flags flying over the building to celebrate countries then represented at Mirny: the Soviet Union, Britain, Czechoslovakia, East Germany, France and Hungary. I found a 'People's artist' busily drawing scenes of life at Mirny. He told me that he was here for a few weeks to record on canvas as much as he could.

Asking after dinner where I was to lay my head for the night, I was led to a twin-bedded room normally occupied by senior members of the expedition. My roommate turned out to be A.P. Kibalin, deputy head of the outgoing crew. The furnishings were more reminiscent of a flat in Moscow than an Antarctic station. Interested to compare this comfortable room with the rooms for lowlier personnel, I wandered into a neighbouring hut. Two or three men were housed in a room, each with his own bed, writing-desk and cupboard. Hot-water radiators were fed from an electric immersion heater, and there was an anthracite stove as back-up in case of power failure. The walls were papered and hung with landscape paintings, and there was a carpet on the floor. There was a dial telephone and a public address loudspeaker that carried announcements, local news and Radio Moscow programmes. By my standards, this was sheer luxury. On some British

30

A 'management'-class bedroom at Mirny

expeditions, men lived in conditions resembling those of stabled horses—though a horse is given a place of its own, while the men were stacked in bunks.

Exploring further the following day, I found a very clean diesel power station supplying about 200 kilowatts, a figure which gives a fair idea of the size of the establishment. From a large balloon-launching building two radiosonde balloons were sent up daily and tracked by radar. The meteorologists had a well-equipped laboratory of continuously recording instruments. I went over the cosmic ray station, geomagnetism station and the auroral radar; found the radio propagation station busily taping *sputnik* signals; and saw four seismographs, well-seated on a patch of bedrock, and an ionosphere sounder buzzing away at the command of a large chronometer. In short, it was the best-equipped Antarctic research station that I had seen. I was told that 92 men would stay at Mirny during the coming winter. That made the place almost urban in character. The last thing I myself wanted, in this land of wide open spaces, was to live in a town, so I was glad to be destined for a 14-man station.

Six pigs lived at Mirny in a wooden pigsty. At first I thought this bizarre, but it was explained that the pigs were fed entirely on kitchen scraps, and provided fresh pork and bacon for special occasions. It

31

was the only recycling system I had ever seen in Antarctica—simple, economical and effective.

On 20 January, I was asked to move out of the twin bedroom to make way for A.F. Anikin, Kibalin's replacement. I found myself in a comfortable room with Nikolay Zheleznov, a 33-year-old journalist from TASS, the Soviet news agency, and Ivan Chernov, a flight radio operator. I had got to know Chernov on *Estonia* and had helped him to study English. English is the international language of civil aviation, so he could not fly with Aeroflot abroad until he had passed a stiff examination in the use of air traffic control language. We practised together; I read out the control tower phrases and he responded. He taped the exchanges so that he could work on pronunciation. Walking past the window of his room days later, I heard a familiar voice (my own) saying: 'Aeroflot two seven niner, taxi to your left, hold short of runway, report ready for take-off.'

In return for my tuition, Chernov taught me the morse code in Russian, which later proved useful. As an amateur radio enthusiast, he said that he had made about 750 contacts in 70 countries.

One evening I was playing music on my tape-recorder when an older man came in. Hearing that it was a church organ concert, he said, 'You don't believe in all that God stuff, do you?' I did not reply to the question, but pointed out that the church organ was my favourite musical instrument. He quietly scoffed. Then Chernov arrived from next door and sat down, clearly enraptured by the music and, like me, unconcerned about what anyone else read into it.

As well as Zheleznov from TASS, there was Viktor Koshevoy, a 41-year-old TASS photo-reporter. He proudly showed me a photograph that he had taken of the Head of State, Nikita Khrushchev, attending a reception at the US Embassy in Moscow for mourners after the assassination of President John F. Kennedy. At home, he said, he had a framed photo of himself with Khrushchev.

Among the staff at Mirny was an interpreter, 38-year-old Roman Tukhanin, here to help visitors from foreign ships. As I got to know him, he frequently turned our conversation towards politics, lecturing me on the merits of communism and the need for workers of the world to unite. I said that there were only about 200,000 members of the Communist Party in Britain, so I believed that our revolution was unlikely. He reminded me that at the time of the October revolution, there were only 120,000 members of the Bolshevik party in all of Russia. He had a point.

Tukhkanin asked me to teach him to swear in English, insisting that I should include the most obscene phrases I knew. Having served on the lower deck in the Royal Navy, I knew a good many. At the end

32

Piotr Shumsky

of the lesson he said, 'I thought so—Russians swear much worse than anybody else.'

One fine day I went for a walk over the sea ice with Shumsky, the Frenchmen and two East German physicists. There were 14 small islands within easy walking distance. The first two that we came upon were covered in nesting Adélie penguins. Bauer killed four of them with the intention of stuffing them to take home.

The third island served as Mirny's cemetery. Here there were coffins or memorial plaques to 14 members of the expedition—a stark reminder of the risks of living in Antarctica. One massive slab recorded the deaths of eight men in a fire in 1960.[1] Fire is the over-

33

Mirny cemetery

riding hazard for people living in huts buried under snow. At Mirny almost everyone was at risk, and keenly aware of it. Two graves were of men killed when an ice cliff calved and fell on *Lena*, a sistership of *Ob*. One man, who had been Shumsky's assistant at the time, succumbed to pneumonia after working for hours in a snow pit at a temperature of –52°C. Another drowned when his tractor fell through fast ice, and yet another was lost in a crevasse accident.

The largest of the off-shore islands was Haswell Island, rising to a height of 93 metres. Shumsky related how, in 1957, he had found in a cairn a note, dated 1946, claiming all land in sight as American territory. The note was signed by John H. Roscoe, a member of the US Navy Operation 'Highjump' of 1946–47.

The air temperature during our walk was so warm (about +2°C) that we stripped to the waist. In normal weather, I noticed that Russians had their own ideas about polar clothing. I had brought from home the clothing normally worn by members of British expeditions. This consisted of an outer garment of thin but finely woven wind-proof material. Under this we wore as many sweaters as necessary to cope with varying temperatures. The Russians, in contrast, wore black leather outer garments or a heavily padded parka. On many occasions people pointed to my outfit saying, 'Too thin, you will need more here.' I stopped short of protesting that this was the warmest part of

34

Antarctica that I had worked in. However, I was given a pair of leather garments and came to love the comfort they provided both outdoors and in. I was also given a pair of soft felt boots known as 'Farewell Youth', because at home they are worn only by old people. At times I preferred wearing my own heavy ski/mountain boots. I was told that such boots were known as 'Adenauer's Smile', in reference to Konrad Adenauer, Former Chancellor of the Federal Republic of Germany, who brought his country into the North Atlantic Treaty Organization, an act deplored by Moscow.

I spent time begging for various instruments that I would need, because nobody could tell me what might or might not be available at Novolazarevskaya. Shumsky was kind enough to search out a microscope for studying ice crystals, and I scrounged a barograph from the meteorologists. This rather undignified search for the tools of my trade was necessary because, before leaving home, it had proved impossible to find out exactly what the Russians had available. Having normally worn skis while travelling on snow, I asked Somov about borrowing some. He replied that they had none because sastrugi made skiing impossible. This brought home to me that Soviet expeditions relied exclusively on tractors of various kinds to move anywhere. In a private transaction I paid £10 for a pair of skis from Manfred Buttenberg, an East German scientist on his way home.

One evening I was invited by two doctors to a party in the 'hospital', together with a cook, a carpenter, a diesel mechanic and a pilot. Three days earlier, the doctors had taken out a man's appendix and said that they did several such operations a year.

A large jar was tabled containing a fermenting liquid made of apples, oranges and blueberries. The alcohol content, I was told, was 'only 40 per cent'. It was decanted into a bottle and served in round-bottomed glasses, presumably to encourage swigging rather than sipping. The newly operated appendix patient came in from the three-bed recovery ward, and he too was pressed to drink.

Ever since *Ob* had reached the fast ice, she had been breaking a channel to shorten the distance to Mirny before unloading her cargo. However, this involved patiently backing and charging the ice, and the ship only advanced about 1 km each day. Unloading could not be done in daytime, because warm temperatures made the surface too slushy for tractors. Every night, three heavy tractors made the five-hour journey to the ship, each one towing an empty sledge. At the ship, 20 tonnes of cargo were loaded on the sledge for the return journey.

Meanwhile Shumsky and Bauer were waiting for a flight inland that required an aircraft with a longer range than the Li-2, thus an Il-12 (weighing 17 tonnes) or Il-14 (weighing 18 tonnes). However, one of these aircraft was having an engine changed, while the another was being fitted with a new wing.

The parked aircraft beside the runways gave a false impression of the number of machines in flying condition. There was one Il-12, two Il-14 and two Li-2. In retirement there were four Li-2, one Antonov-2 (An-2) biplane and three Mil Mi-4 helicopters.

Shumsky and the Frenchmen finally took off for Vostok in an Il-14 on 26 January. Vostok is 1550 km inland (about half the distance to the South Pole), 3500 metres above sea level and six hours flying time from Mirny. The plan was for the party to pursue their ice-movement studies by accompanying a major convoy of seven heavy tractors returning to Mirny after delivering supplies to Vostok.

Having revealed to Chief Pilot Boris Minkov that I myself was a licensed pilot (though of minimal experience), I was invited on a flight to seek out fresh water to refill *Estonia*'s tanks. I was not quite sure what this entailed, until we flew from one iceberg to another looking for melt ponds that were sometimes found in hollows. After a leisurely tour around Drygalski Island and nearly as far as the Shackleton Ice Shelf, we found a modest pool of water on a small iceberg and notified the ship.

Chief pilot B.A. Minkov

36

Flying with Russians, I found, was delightfully informal. As with my earlier flight, nobody wore a seat-belt and I spent the whole time in the cockpit, including take-off and landing. With an empty Li-2, the crew were in a playful mood and, as a joke, caused Minkov literally to hit the ceiling by pushing the control column abruptly forward while he was walking aft to relieve himself. He was not amused.

Next day the transport department learned that I was not only a pilot but also held a driver's licence. A driver's licence was in those days uncommon in the Soviet Union, so they asked if I would drive a tractor because, in the midst of the handover, they were short of drivers. I was checked out on a Chelyabinsk S-100B tractor, and allowed to go solo after half an hour. The tractor weighed 13 tonnes and hauled a gigantic steel sledge, weighing 8 tonnes and having a 31-square-metre loading platform. On it were 20 tonnes of cargo, making it certainly the heaviest vehicle I had ever driven. I spent the morning driving a working party around camp ferrying stores, which involved reversing the sledge into awkward places. Late in the day I set out in a convoy of six tractors to drive to *Ob*.

While grinding along, I was concerned to see the old Li-2 cruising around with only one ski down, and that pointing downwards at a 45° angle. However, after violent elevator push-pulls by the pilots, the tail rising and falling abruptly, the second ski came down and both were level. Experience tells, and they landed safely.

It took five hours of driving at full speed, 3 knots, to reach the ship because of a long detour made necessary by cracks in the ice. 'What a beautiful ice ship,' I wrote in my diary later. The bow plating, I was told, was of special steel 30-mm thick covering closely-spaced frames.

I learned that *Ob* was carrying 1965 tonnes of cargo destined for Mirny, whereas *Estonia* had brought only 64 tonnes. Leaving the crew to load my sledge, I was invited into the cabin of oceanographer Ilya Romanov, given half a tumbler-full of cognac, and fed. Afterwards I was invited to use his private bathroom, where there was a large bath and water to fill it. Clean for the first time in weeks, I set off for Mirny at 0100 in company with another tractor. Driving in pairs was routine, so that we could help each other if one got bogged down in soft snow.

The ice was covered with deep slushy snow, under which there was water, and under that—we prayed—solid ice. Our tractors frequently broke through into the water, which was alarming because we knew we might be dropping through into the ocean. A driver had lost his life in this way in 1956. By chance, the event was filmed and I had seen the film. It happened so quickly that the driver had no time to jump off the tractor. Another driver had been lost the same way at Molodezhnaya.

I was told that the underlying ice was only 1.1 metres thick and that it was becoming thinner by about 10 cm per week. Each time one of us got bogged down, we strung a steel cable between the tractors and pulled in tandem to a harder surface. The coupling and uncoupling was a sweaty procedure, because we wore heavy clothing designed for sitting still on the tractor for hours. Just as I was crossing the tide cracks to shore at Mirny, the tail of my sledge slid sideways, ending up at a 45° angle. I was terrified of being dragged backwards and tipped over, so ungallantly handed the tractor over to a professional. He failed to budge the sledge, and it was eventually pulled out backwards. Luckily the events were watched by E.A. Zimin, the head of transport, who was quick to say that I was not to blame and should retire to bed. I had been on my feet for 25 hours.

After five hours of sleep, I was off again with another set of drivers. At *Ob* my sledge was the first to be loaded. Just after the hundredth barrel of fuel was put on it, the ice cracked under the sledge and one runner dropped 30 cm. I had parked the tractor 50 metres away to spread the load. There was nothing to be done but back up the tractor, couple the sledge and drive forward. It was a heart-stopping moment. However, as I pulled away, the crew cheered and I felt that my standing had risen a notch or two.

The most alarming thing on the six-hour return journey was crossing cracks bridged over with nothing more than two railway sleepers, one for each track. I recalled that a colleague in 1951, having unexpectedly plunged into the sea, saved his own life by stabbing his sheath knife into an ice floe and hauling himself out. Preparing to follow his example through these ponderous crossings, I stood on the tractor with dagger in hand. 'They don't leave much of a safety factor,' I wrote in my diary.

I told Somov that the cracks were dangerous for a 13-tonne tractor, and the next night I was pleased to find him inspecting them in company with Maksutov, Zimin and five others. They watched with concern as each of the tractors crossed. On my return with a load, the biggest crack had four more beams across it. At Mirny, I was towed up the steep snow slope to deposit my 75th tonne of fuel.

As days fled by, I felt that I ought to take home a first-hand account of all the Soviet stations. After some heavy hints, Somov said that I could fly to Vostok the next day. Perhaps it was a reward for risking my neck on the fast ice. However, a blizzard blew up and instead there was a day of rest.

For the men in camp and not otherwise engaged, a full-length feature film was shown every evening in the dining-room. Most were Soviet films. In contrast to American films, which seemed to glorify wealth, Soviet films glorified humble hard-working citizens. The hero was a soldier, a crane driver or a truck driver. The films were entertaining but the message was always the same: labour brings its own rewards—the respect of one's colleagues rather than wealth.

Wealth by Soviet standards, perhaps the ownership of a car, was sometimes featured as a carrot for hard work. However, whatever the official line, the most popular films were American. There were quite a number resulting from exchanges or gifts made in the course of goodwill visits by American ships and aircraft. The first I saw was about the Yukon gold rush in 1849, and there was lots of shooting. This was refreshing for the Russians because, in their experience, news of crime at home was generally suppressed as being incompatible with the myth of harmony in a worker's paradise. Reference to American films was invariably accompanied by mock shooting, a sad commentary on what was perceived to be their main ingredient.

Saturday night was bath night. The bath house was attached to the power station and made use of waste heat from the generators. A steam room contained large hand-basins and hot water was unlimited. The atmosphere was festive and the men used strands of old rope or loofahs to scrub their friends. Bath night was invariably followed by a well-lubricated party.

4

The Coldest Place on Earth

All the Novolazarevskaya crew were now ashore, and they had spent the last few days rolling fuel drums from sledges into storage depots, a back-breaking job. I joined them for a day and was impressed by their cheerfulness. Jokes and laughter constantly filled the air. The work would have continued the next day but I was saved from further drudgery by flying to Vostok.

Woken at 0530, I flew in the Il-12 with the same aircrew as on the fresh-water flight. Minkov was in command and others served as co-pilot, navigator and radio operator. I recorded the names of each one and asked about his total flying time since qualifying. Between them they had flown 51,000 hours, a reassuring total. The aircraft carried a tonne of cargo and three passengers.

Flying at 100–300 metres over the snow surface all the way, the pilots were able to follow tracks from the tractor train that had driven from Mirny to Vostok in November. Passing over Komsomolskaya, a weather station occupied only in summer, they dropped a barrel of anti-freeze through a pair of bomb doors in the floor. A normal barrel would have broken on impact but this one was specially designed for airdrops; it had concave ends and three steel hoops to prevent impact damage.

After more than six hours in the air, we touched down on the smoothest snow runway I had ever landed on. Vostok was the southernmost Soviet station, the highest station operated by any nation in Antarctica, and the coldest occupied place on Earth. It was of unique scientific interest owing to its proximity to the South Geomagnetic Pole.

We had arrived on a normal summer day—the temperature was −44°C. The whole population of 20 or so turned out to greet us. Minkov stopped the engine on the cargo-door side while leaving the other engine turning. Standing in the propeller slipstream would have caused instant frostbite. Everyone helped to unload and it took only a few minutes, after which the aircraft took off. I was invited to stay overnight, so made my way to the station building.

Unloading an Ilyushin-12 at Vostok

Meteorologists define a desert as an area where the average annual rainfall (or its equivalent in snow) is less than 100 millimetres. Vostok was well within that definition. Yet paradoxically, I thought, the desert we were standing on was part of the world's largest body of fresh water—albeit in solid form.

Whereas coastal stations built on snow generally become buried within a couple of years, here at Vostok some of the buildings were only half buried six years after they were built. Inside, I found Shumsky and the French party preparing for their journey back to Mirny. Then an American, John Jacobs, introduced himself. Like me, he was an exchange scientist and was to remain at Vostok for the year. He had flown here two weeks earlier from McMurdo, the main American station in McMurdo Sound. Jacobs arrived with 19 tonnes of equipment in two LC-130 Hercules loads, together with a gang of 40 US Navy 'Seabees' to build two huts for him. They also erected two very tall masts for his research on natural radio emissions and solar proton fluxes. All was now built and the Seabees were back at McMurdo. I could not help feeling for the Russians, all of whose supplies and equipment had to be dragged by tractors all the way from the coast.

With scant regard for local sensitivities, the Seabees had hung a very large American flag from the top of one of the masts. The other

41

Vostok station

mast wore smaller flags of our Soviet hosts, together with those of Czechoslovakia, East Germany and France; also an American flag of a more diplomatic size.

Jacobs had arrived with a lavish supply of books, films and taped music. He said he had undergone a six-week course in Russian at the US Army School of Languages in Monterey, California. However, I wrote in my diary, 'He is not up to much.' I had by that time been immersed in colloquial Russian for two months, but was not up to much either.

Next I was introduced to two East German geodesists who were there for a few weeks to determine the precise position of Vostok by using a geodetic theodolite to make star sights. They had set up the instrument 100 metres from the station, but in spite of the distance, their observations were affected by vibration from the station's diesel generator. One of them told me that his monthly salary at home was 7000 Deutschmarks whereas here in the Antarctic it was 30,000. He would arrive home with a small fortune. No wonder, I thought, that many of these people come back year after year. When I asked what his wife thought of it all, he said she virtually pushed him back south, because after one year they could afford a bigger apartment and after a second year they could buy a Trabant. Carry on long enough and it could become a Mercedes.

A Czech physicist was operating a neutron monitor surrounded by seven tonnes of lead to keep out stray radiation; the same man looked after a meson telescope. Other research programmes were in meteorology, aerology, geomagnetism, earth currents, aurora and the ionosphere. The whole programme was to be managed by a wintering party of only 14 men: the station leader with seven scientists and a doctor, cook, radio operator, electrician, diesel engineer and vehicle mechanic.

Contrasting with the 200-kilowatt output of the Mirny power station, Vostok had generators producing only 11 kilowatts. Enquiring how they could keep warm in winter with so little power, I was told that sufficient heat was recovered from the exhaust and the cooling circuit of the generator. However, they admitted that because of a fuel shortage, the available power was half what they really needed.

Meals were better than at Mirny. I suppose it was to compensate for the climate and isolation of Vostok. Evidently working outside in winter must be extremely stressful. The lowest temperature ever recorded here (or anywhere else on our planet) was –89°C. In these temperatures, they explained, steel can shatter like glass, petrol can extinguish fire like water and diesel fuel can be cut with a saw. To liquify their fuel, each 200-litre drum had to be brought into the warmth of the power station two weeks before it was opened. For months, men could venture outside only by wearing heavy clothing and a face mask.

I had been feeling the effects of altitude ever since arriving at Vostok: headache, nausea and lassitude. The aircrew had warned that this would last at least 24 hours and, although I was given a comfortable bed, I hardly slept. When I awoke and struggled out of bed, I was still suffering and only managed to hold down a small breakfast. Venturing outside, however, was a tonic. The temperature was –40°C but the air was filled with tiny ice crystals glinting in the sunlight. This effect is known as 'diamond dust'—and one might almost believe it was. A ghostly halo ringed the sun so that the whole scene had a sublime beauty that moved me to tears. In seconds, however, the tears turned to ice.

The French party were calibrating their survey instruments and preparing the vehicles that would take them on the long journey to Mirny. The heaviest tractor, called a Kharkovchanka, was powered by a 520-hp supercharged V-12 diesel engine and weighed 35 tonnes. Inside were several rooms giving a total floor area of about 30 square metres, making it bigger than many a Soviet apartment. In the largest room there was an anthracite stove, six bunks and a double-burner propane stove for cooking. Opening off this was a radio room, Captain's office and an aircraft-type toilet. The machine could tow a

Kharkovchanka at Vostok

sledge of about 65 tonnes, the actual amount depending on the soft-
ness of the snow. Kharkovchankas have worked at altitudes up to
4000 metres and temperatures down to −70°C.

Having travelled in many crevassed areas, generally using a pair of
skis to spread my body weight, my first thought was that I would not
like to drive across a snow bridge while sitting on 35 tonnes of steel.
However, I was assured that very few Kharkovchankas had fallen into
crevasses. The explanation must be that any crevasse wide enough to
swallow a vehicle 8.5 metres long would have a conspicuously sag-
ging snow bridge that would alert the driver before he reached it.

The other kind of tractor was an ATT Tyagach[1] that weighed only
25 tonnes and was powered by a 420-hp diesel engine. It was an
artillery tractor widely used by the Soviet army. Configured as a
truck, it had a driver's cab at the front and an open loading platform
that could take 20 fuel drums. In addition it could tow up to 50
tonnes, depending on the consistency of the snow. Some of the ATT
machines had a caboose built on the loading platform; inside were six
bunks and an anthracite stove.

I was consumed with admiration both for the 35-tonne and also the
25-tonne machines. What other vehicles, I wondered, could ply this
route twice a year under extreme weather with soft snow surfaces in
tractor-trains hauling hundreds of tonnes of cargo. Without a load,

Tyagach tractor at Vostok

both types could cruise at speeds up to 30 km/hr, though driving over sastrugi gave a very bumpy roller-coaster kind of ride.

When I had recovered from 24 hours of altitude sickness, it was time to return to Mirny. To have had this opportunity of seeing the coldest place on Earth was a very special privilege. I had a quick lunch, then two aircraft flew in. After helping to unload the first, I waved my hosts goodbye and clambered into the second. It was an Il-14, identical from the outside but more powerful than the Il-12.

While American aircraft invariably used rockets to assist take-off at this altitude, the Russian pilot just opened the throttles and waited. During the take-off run I was grabbed by the radio operator and navigator, who yelled 'Come aft!' We ran to the back of the cargo cabin until the nose-ski rose and the machine staggered into the thin air. At this altitude, a loaded Ilyushin required a take-off run of 3 km. At sea level, by contrast, not even the heaviest aircraft ever built needed that much runway. To be on the safe side, the Vostok runway was 3.8 km long and 70 metres wide.

I sat with the crew as before. The pilot, M.V. Kostayev, had 12,000 flying hours under his belt, sported a pointed beard and reminded me of some jolly buccaneer. During the war he had been a dive-bomber pilot. He told me that by Soviet standards he was a capitalist, by which he meant that, by comparison with ordinary citizens, senior

Ilyushin-12 fighting to get airborne in the thin air at Vostok, the highest station in Antarctica (3500 metres above sea level)

pilots were highly paid. This led us into a calm discussion of the merits of communism; capitalism was assumed to be devoid of merits. The radio operator, P.V. Boiko, wore a sour expression on his face but proved to be delightful company while exercising his few words of English.

Following tractor tracks on the flight was mesmerizing, so some of the crew took catnaps. When still 300 km from Mirny, we lost the sun and flew into a whiteout. This is a condition in which daylight is diffused by multiple reflection between the snow surface and an overcast sky. Contrasts vanish and pilots can no longer distinguish the snow surface. There have been many flying accidents in whiteouts, though Soviet airmen were more vigilant than most. We lost the tractor tracks and flew on instruments. I could sense tension rising in the cockpit as the windscreen iced up. With 150 km to go, we ran into solid cloud and severe icing. Sitting between the pilots, the engineer switched on all the electrical de-icers. Anxious glances were made to the leading edge of the wing to check on ice build-up. As the de-icers took effect, great sheets of ice peeled off and new ice took their place. There were bangs and clatters as ice flew off the spinners and hit the side of the fuselage. It was good to be sitting up front to watch the crew engage in rapid-fire teamwork.

To compound the problem, Mirny was within 1700 km of the South Magnetic Pole, making the compass almost unreadable. Indeed, given the choice, the needle would have pointed downwards at an angle of 78° to the horizontal. Every couple of minutes the navigator called out the distance to go according to his dead reckoning. As the altitude of the ice sheet fell away, we kept 200 metres above the snow surface that we could not see. Finally, we broke cloud very close to Mirny and landed on the short runway, the co-pilot handling the controls while the Captain worked the throttles. On the way in, I saw five tractors on the way to *Ob*. There were large cracks and ice-free pools round some of the icebergs.

Blowing 13 m/sec [25 knots] and snowing today, so the tractor drivers must be having a hell of a time.[2]

Arriving in the dining-room, we were given a late supper while the rest of the population were watching a film.

The next day I joined the Novolazarevskaya crew in a working party that was unloading fuel drums from sledges as they arrived from *Ob*. There was a 40-knot blizzard blowing, so we became soaked and plastered with snow. At supper an old man chatted with me and introduced himself as Andrey Medvedev, the Mirny airport manager. Sensing that here was a man with a story, I asked about his experiences. He had worked on some of the earliest Soviet drifting research stations on the Arctic Ocean pack ice and was now at the end of his third winter in the Antarctic. His sport was parachuting, and at one time he had been parachute-jumping champion of the USSR. Asked how many jumps that meant, he said he had done 1336, some from as high as 8000 metres and involving a 40-second free fall. For those, he said, he had to wear a face mask. I asked if his main parachute had ever failed to open. 'Yes,' he said, 'I have had to use my reserve chute about ten times.' In his spare time he had been a light aircraft pilot, a mechanic and a photographer, and he was still a correspondent for *Sovetskaya Rossiya*. I wrote in my diary, 'What an interesting lot of people we have here.'

That night the film was *See you in Las Vegas*. It had been presented to the crew of a Li-2 that called in at Mawson, the main Australian research station situated some 1300 km to the west of Mirny. Venturing outside afterwards, I was knocked down by a 50-knot blizzard.

The new boys learning quickly about snowdrifts, now filling all hollows. To get to meals we have to struggle up hill and down dale in drifts up to our knees.

Andrey Medvedev, airport manager and parachutist

It was now 10 February and my time at Mirny was drawing to a close. Maksutov asked me to drive a tractor with two sledges to *Ob* and to move on board. I was third in a convoy of six. No return driver was needed because the tractor was to be put on board. Some people rode in greater comfort than others—Somov was seated in the cabin of a superannuated helicopter lashed to a sledge.

The sea ice was evidently more rotten than before. The first tractor broke through into 40 centimetres of water before coming to rest on the ice below. Then four tractors including my own followed it into a cold bath. I was less shaken by the event itself than by the thought that the machine might have continued to the seabed with me on it. By this time it was quite dark and there was a fine display of the aurora overhead. One by one we rescued each other and, after $2^{1}/_{2}$ hours of hard labour, the train moved on.

The wind was still high and there was surface drifting, so it was no picnic sitting up there on the throne for 7 hours [none of the tractors had cabs].

One by one we made it to the ship. I arrived at 0600, staggered

48

straight to my allotted bunk and fell into a deep sleep. It had been one of the hardest days of my life. Yet everyone had done what had to be done and, amazingly, there was as much laughter as sorrow.

Ob was a diesel-electric freighter built in Holland for the Soviet Government and was the best-known of all Russian polar vessels. At 7500 tons gross and a loaded displacement of 12,600 tonnes, she was nearly twice the size of *Estonia*. All told, she had covered 780,000 km on nine Antarctic cruises, sailed in every ocean, visited 22 countries and carried 210,000 tonnes of cargo and 3300 passengers. Since *Ob* often spent northern summers at sea in the Arctic, her crew saw very little of her home port of Murmansk. Within the last year she had visited the port of London, and also Hull to deliver a cargo of plywood from Leningrad.

I shared a cabin with Mojmír Konečný, the only other foreigner bound for Novolazarevskaya. Mojmír worked for the Geophysical Institute of the Czechoslovak Academy of Sciences and planned to study variations in the Earth's magnetic field. A quiet and reserved but likeable young man, he was born in Moravia and went to school in Brno before moving to Prague in 1958. Married with two children, he proposed to work up his own studies at Novolazarevskaya to obtain a PhD.

Mojmír could speak a few words of English and from the start I felt relaxed with him. If for no other reason, it was because we felt more European than the rest. I was careful never to discuss politics for fear of prejudicing his position. While I could feel that he was not a communist, he was wise enough to accept the rules. One day when I was rebelling over some petty restriction he said, 'Charles, you have not yet learned the first rule of living in a socialist society: never swim against the stream!'

Our cabin was better than those of our colleagues and we were told to eat with the officers; native Russians were consigned below. Here was the same discrimination in favour of foreigners that I had encountered when given the 'management'-class room at Mirny. Mojmír and I were both embarrassed because we wanted to be treated as equal partners in our small community. At the same time we realized that privileged treatment of foreigners was a normal component of Russian courtesy in their own country, so it would be hard to change.

We were pampered. My woolly underwear was brought from the laundry by a lovely lady who apologized for not having the right coloured wool to darn the holes. Up to that time, my practice on expeditions had been to use underwear until it disintegrated, then to start on a new set.

When the engines came to life and the ship vibrated, we knew that

Ob had begun to fight for her freedom from the fast ice. It took three hours of backing and filling to turn through 180° in the channel that the ship herself had cut on the way in. Sixteen hours later we came out of the pack ice and turned west for Molodezhnaya and—sooner or later—Novolazarevskaya.

The ship was equipped with large oceanographic laboratories. Continuous lines of soundings were run with specially-built British-made echo sounders, while *Ob*'s hydrographers made position observations independently from the ship's navigating officer. Stopping at intervals to measure currents, temperature and salinity at various depths right down to the seabed, *Ob* worked her way slowly westwards towards Molodezhnaya. Chief of the marine division of scientists on board was hydrologist Viktor Ledenyev, a young man with wide interests and a surprisingly easy way of discussing everything from American domestic politics to Soviet censorship and the KGB. In science I now found it easy to converse freely and it was rewarding to probe and to learn about the background to his studies. Ledenyev gave me office space on the boat deck and the loan of a calculating machine.

Four days after leaving Mirny we approached Mawson, Australia's main Antarctic base that was named for Sir Douglas Mawson. Mawson, leader of the Australian Antarctic Expedition of 1911–1914 and author of *The Home of the Blizzard*,[3] was the most famous name

Mawson, the principal Australian station

in Australia's Antarctic history. The station was built on a rocky outcrop at the edge of the ice sheet. A steep but smooth ice slope rose behind the base, and in the distance we could see mountains. The ship had no chart of the area and there were many offshore islands, so the approach was tricky. Eventually we dropped anchor off a sheltered cove close to the station. I was invited to the ship's radio room to speak to the base and to interpret for Somov. My first goodwill message on behalf of the Soviet Antarctic Expedition went down well and a boatload of Russians were invited ashore.

Together with A.Z. Vaygachev, one of five hydrographers in the ship, I accompanied Somov ashore with a bundle of hydrographic charts to give to the base, hoping for some local charts in exchange. Ray McMahon, the young leader of the base, said he had none—they were all in the Australian ships. Showing us round, he explained that he had 25 men housed in a variety of separate buildings, all of them constructed directly on ice-scoured bedrock. Several of the buildings had large windows, and there was a library, music room, billiard room and cinema.

'An idyllic spot,' I wrote in my diary. However, I was told that not all days were warm and calm like this one. In the last 12 months they had lost one vehicle that broke through sea ice; one man had died of a cerebral haemorrhage; and the doctor had lost the tips of two fingers during a winter journey in which a field party was buried in their tent under snowdrifts. When they cut their way out, two sleeping bags had been blown away and the party survived only through a forced march to Mawson on a compass bearing in the dark.

Though the buildings were immaculate, the men themselves wore long beards and scruffy clothes. Seven of them had just returned from a long exploratory journey inland with one 13-dog sledge and two Caterpillar tractors. Parked outside the buildings were a jeep, a weasel,[4] a farm tractor, a small snowmobile and four motorcycles, two of them with sidecar. An unmodified Volkswagen 'beetle' bore the number plate *Antarctica 1*. All the wheeled vehicles could be driven south straight onto the steeply-sloping ice ramp because it was snow-free for tens of kilometres inland, an unusual condition for Antarctica. This was due to high winds that bore down from inland, sweeping snow out to sea.

On behalf of Somov I invited Ray McMahon and three others to lunch on board. On coming up the gangway and spotting the first women that they had seen in 15 months, the Australians smothered them with kisses. At that moment, language differences were no barrier to communication. After lunch we were invited to the

Captain's cabin and faced with a second lunch washed down with champagne, vodka and cognac.

Leaving the Australians, who had accepted rather too much hospitality, I went ashore again on the ship's pontoon carrying 10 tonnes of avgas[5] and 33 sightseers. Somov was driven up the ramp to inspect the 'airstrip', an area of bare ice on which Australian and Soviet aircraft have from time to time landed. Later he told me of a harrowing experience some years earlier. Arriving in a Li-2, he and his aircrew landed in a storm. They could not risk attempting to walk down to Mawson, nor could the Australians safely reach them. They secured the aircraft by means of a single steel stake drilled into the ice. For some 20 hours the crew sheltered in the fuselage, while its thousands of rivets creaked and groaned. At intervals, and after an alarming series of lurches, the machine skidded round its stake to align with the changing wind direction. Had it not done so, it could have been flipped on its back.

Seven of us were invited to stay for supper at Mawson, and afterwards most of the Australians came on board and danced with our ladies. When finally they were taken ashore, two of them, both the worse for wear, launched a sailing dinghy and brought the last two Russians aboard.

Several people expressed surprise at how friendly the Australians were. I had heard similar remarks after our visits to Le Havre and Fremantle. While I myself expected the natives to be friendly, I could only guess that Soviet propaganda had led my comrades to expect something less.

Steaming westwards in a calm sea spotted with icebergs, we passed the promontory of Enderby Land. Behind an ice wall that in places was very high, the ice sheet rose in steps punctuated by nunataks and small mountain ranges. The air was magically clear and we must have been seeing mountains that were more than 100 km from the ship. Next we passed Proclamation Island, where on 13 January 1930 Mawson had annexed the area for the British Crown. Now the land is claimed by Australia as part of Australian Antarctic Territory, though the Russians reject this and all other territorial claims throughout Antarctica.

Late in the evening we passed a giant iceberg—about 50 km in length—that must have broken from the Amery Ice Shelf. Its sides were unweathered, suggesting that it was newly calved from its parent. A conspicuous blue band in the cliff face showed that there had been surface melting during a series of warm summers. The Captain, Nikolay Sviridov, told me that the sides were up to 45 metres high. If so, it was the tallest iceberg that I had ever seen.

5

'Party' Meetings

On 17 February we arrived at the edge of fast ice some 15 km north of Molodezhnaya station and began to cut a channel towards the shore. The ice was no more than 0.7 metres thick, but its sticky snow cover meant that the ship made slow progress. In the first 24 hours we hardly made more than 1 kilometre. A Li-2 landed on the ice beside *Ob* to fly Somov to the station.

The next day I was invited ashore on condition that I did not mind sleeping in a tent. I shared the Li-2 with a load of specially-reinforced fuel drums of the type used for free-dropping fuel to tractor traverses. The tent was dome-shaped and spacious, and I shared it with Yury Model, a geologist. Maksutov, who had flown from Mirny, and Somov gave me a guided tour. Molodezhnaya was a new station still under construction but intended to replace Mirny as the principal Soviet base. That year the wintering population was to be 36, of whom 21 would be construction workers. Buildings were spread over a wide area of partially moraine-covered bedrock. Constructed of 'Arbolite', a mixture of wood chips and cement, they were built on stilts to keep the doors clear of snowdrifts. If not totally fire-proof, Arbolite was flame-proof and fire retardant. The disastrous fire at Mirny in 1960 had made people intensely aware of the hazards of wooden huts buried under snow.

The station was built here because there was an unlimited supply of fresh water in lakes, one of them 29 metres deep. The lakes froze over in winter, but water was extracted from under the ice by means of sub-mersible pumps and heated pipes. No other Antarctic station was blessed with such a bountiful supply of melt-water from the ice sheet.

Having time on our hands while *Ob* was breaking her way towards the shore, I asked to visit Hayes Glacier, an ice stream 15 km east of the station. With luck, I could measure its rate of movement in a few days. A young glacial geomorphologist, Yury Konovalov, borrowed a GAZ-47 Vezdekhod, a 3.7-tonne all-terrain tracked vehicle, in which we drove off with Nikolay Tretyakov, a young surveyor, and a

An 'Arbolite' building under construction at Molodezhnaya station

Russian theodolite. After a bumpy ride over bare ice we reached the 8-km wide glacier, enjoyed a picnic lunch, measured a baseline and took angles to some conspicuous seracs in the middle of the glacier. Meanwhile, Konovalov spent two hours dealing with a blocked fuel line in the vehicle. Finishing our work by evening, we stopped to admire a spectacular panorama of the giant glacier and a score of icebergs that it had spawned into the sea.

That night my tent-mate told me that his father was a former Bolshevik journalist, who in his early years had worked underground. From 1907 to 1917, he was a political refugee in the United States. After the revolution he returned to Russia, worked with Lenin and was at one time editor of the Communist Party newspaper *Izvestiya*. Now aged 74, his father enjoyed a specially large pension because of his long service as a communist.

Once every two weeks, Radio Moscow broadcast messages to one of the four Soviet stations from the men's families at home. When our turn came, everyone crowded round the loudspeakers, each listening intently to catch the sometimes garbled voices of his wife and children.

Someone remarked that it was like hearing voices from another world. It was, and they were...

On 25 February, *Ob* put to sea for a rendezvous with *Apsheron*, a tanker of the Black Sea fleet based in Odessa. *Apsheron*'s principal task was to refuel the Soviet whaling fleet, but *Ob* had arranged in advance to replenish her bunkers while the tanker was in the vicinity.

Resuming her icebreaking, *Ob* finally secured against an icefoot 11 days after starting to cut her channel. The icefoot was four metres high, an ideal height for unloading cargo straight onto sledges. *Ob* brought mail from *Apsheron* and—that evening—I joyfully buried myself in three letters from home and seven others. Never in my life had I hungered for news as much.

The Il-12 arrived from Mirny with a few passengers. The pilot, V.F. Melnikov, brought the awful news that there had been a fatal accident near Mirny. After a tractor party did not return to base when expected, the Il-14 was launched to search for them. The aircraft found tracks and followed them to where they ended in a black hole. The tractor had left a known safe trail to make a short cut to the station. A snow bridge gave way and the tractor fell 23 metres. The 23-year-old driver Anatoly Shcheglov was killed, though his two passengers survived. It was 16 hours before the survivors were brought to the surface.

Ever since 3 January, a 15-man group led by the geophysicist Andrey Kapitsa had been slowly making its way along a circuitous route from Vostok towards Molodezhnaya.[1] Using two Kharkovchankas and one Tyagach, the party were penetrating an unexplored region to within 900 km of the South Pole. Their route lay through the Pole of Inaccessibility, a small area calculated to be the farthest from any point on the coastline. There, I was told, a formerly occupied station was adorned with a gypsum bust of Lenin. Throughout the journey the party was measuring ice thickness by seismic sounding, and also the height of the ice surface by geodetic levelling.

I was asked to go on a flight to scout Kapitsa's proposed route from a point far inland to their journey's end at Molodezhnaya. At the same time, we would airdrop drums of fuel because the party's stocks were low. However, on reaching the aircraft and contacting Kapitsa by radio, he reported that we might not find the tractors because they were in fog. So the pilot gave up and returned to base. Before turning-in, there was a lively argument between Melnikov and Somov. Somov, aware that the tractors could not move until they received more fuel, maintained that we should have flown anyway, asking the traverse party to send up rockets or smoke through the haze to pinpoint their position.

I bunked with the aircrew in a tiny three-metre-square room. The morning brought snow and high winds, so I walked to *Ob* with the

Welding keels onto sledge runners to combat side-skidding

intention of getting a book to read. I learned that during my absence, 12 of my colleagues had flown to Novolazarevskaya to begin the take-over from last year's crew. Wondering why only Prokopiev and I were left behind, I soon found the reason—we were needed as tractor drivers. During the next 13 hours, I made eight trips between the ship and various cargo dumps carrying prefabricated Arbolite panels. Next day I took five more. The last bit of the trail into the station included traversing a steep slope with a cliff at the bottom. More than once the loaded sledge skidded downslope, dragging me and my tractor perilously close to the cliff. I was not the only driver to have had a fright, because later in the day I saw a man welding a shallow keel onto the underside of the sledge runners to prevent side-skids.

Another time, ready to pull away from the ship with 25 tonnes behind me, I let out the clutch with a bang. This was always needed to get the train moving. However, this time I had mistakenly selected reverse gear, and there was a crash as 40 tonnes of tractor and sledge slammed into the side of the ship. I quickly selected first gear and pulled away before anyone could see my red face. Later I surreptitiously inspected the dent in the ship's plating—a lasting memorial to my clumsiness. However, nobody mentioned it.

It was 4 March before the weather was right for the flight to Kapitsa's party. Somov and I were the only passengers. After 730 km

Huddling beside their two Kharkovchanka and one Tyagach in an unexplored part of the continent, Kapitsa's group watch our Ilyushin-14 free-dropping needed barrels of diesel fuel

we reached the target, a forlorn little speck of humanity in this ocean of ice. We dropped five drums of fuel, a parachute-load of spare parts, and mail.

I never met Kapitsa during the expedition. It was not until 36 years later that I met him for the first time—in Cambridge. Recalling the event, he remembered every detail and said that some of the fuel drums had burst on impact because Melnikov was flying too high.

On landing back at base after a long flight, it was the duty of the navigator to drain a litre of fluid from the aircraft's de-icing system. Unlike some de-icing fluids, this was pure alcohol (ethanol). Once indoors, it was served to the aircrew and passengers. It seemed an admirable way of winding down from the stresses of the flight. Tradition has it that the alcohol must be diluted to reduce its concentration to the latitude where it is served. Thus only at the South Pole (90°S) would it be drunk at 90 per cent. The navigator, A.S. Bertsinsky, related how it was served to an American airman at a Russian air base during the war. Unused to liquor that strong, the American knocked it back, spluttered, and said, 'Gasoline, you bastards!'

Back in the ship, I saw a notice announcing the time of the next

57

The author

Communist Party meeting. It ended with the words: 'All are welcome'. Asking whether that included me, I was told: 'Of course.' Attendance was compulsory for all party members off watch, but voluntary for non-members and for the expedition staff. It was the first of a number of Party meetings that I attended. Each time I was struck by how much they had in common with church services back in England. The 'sermon' began with a text from the 'bible'—in this case the works of Lenin—which was then interpreted in a fairly orthodox way by the speaker. Lenin's works were so prolific that they provided scope for a wide choice of subject matter. Another thing they had in common with some of the sermons I have endured was that they were boring.

Meanwhile the unloading continued. A posted 'wall newspaper' reported that there were in all 1935 tonnes to be unloaded at Molodezhnaya. I worked the day shift, from 0800 to 2000. Afterwards, tea was served in Somov's cabin as we discussed the expedition's plans and progress. He showed me Kapitsa's monthly situation report, which read just like my own 'sitreps' during the years I worked with

Ob's wall newspaper for 11 March 1964 at Molodezhnaya. The small print at the top right of the sheet admonishes: 'Workers of the world unite!' The headline reads: 'Today by 12 o'clock we have unloaded 1655 tonnes... There remains to be unloaded 280 tonnes of fuel oil'. Among the news from other stations is the day's temperature at Vostok: –69.8°C (the minus sign was considered superfluous)

the Americans. In a relaxed mood, Somov admitted that he smoked 30 cigarettes a day. If every packet were stacked one on top of the other, he lamented, the pile would rise to 165 metres, the height of the Moscow University skyscraper.

On 6 March, I was invited to join a Li-2 flight to look for crevasses on Kapitsa's proposed tractor route. As before, I was impressed by the professionalism of the 6-man crew. The third I had flown with, they had between them logged 36,500 hours in the air. In a $6^1/_2$-hour flight we saw many crevasses and did our best to plot them on a map, though our positions were totally dependent on the navigator's dead-reckoning. A satisfactory lunch was provided on the flight: fish, bread, butter and coffee.

Both in the ship and on shore there seemed to be a touch of France in the frequency of handshaking. It was warming to see how people who had lived in close quarters for months on end would, on returning after an absence of a few days, shake hands with everyone.

There was an orgy of handshaking on International Women's Day (8 March). Everyone dressed in their best and I sensed that there were political overtones to the occasion. There were several prepared speeches congratulating the working women of the USSR, particularly *Ob*'s 30 women, on their contribution to 'the building of socialism'. A present of chocolates and perfume was made to each of them in turn. These ceremonies were followed by a concert, dancing and plenty of liquor. At a private party afterwards I was drawn into a political discussion with the Chief Engineer Nikolay Afanasyev—much to the delight of the others present. He was a bit under the weather and kept on interrupting my rather laboured Russian. The Third Engineer came to my defence, saying, 'Hear him out—let the Englishman have his say.' Soon bonhomie overcame any potential for serious debate. Afanasyev leant over and said, 'I'll bet you don't know who runs the Party in this ship.' You could have heard a pin drop as everyone waited for my response. I decided to chance it, so dug him in the ribs and said, 'You do!' Peals of laughter showed that I had scored a bull's-eye.

Next day I asked Afanasyev if he would show me over the engine room. After we had shared a bottle of white wine in his cabin, this was agreed. He subscribed to the general assumption that I was a spy, and said, 'No cameras allowed in the engine room—much very secret material.' On seeing the place I concluded that the 'secret' was simply a far from immaculate engine room undergoing repairs. Russians, particularly party members, liked to show their best side to foreigners.

After the tour we returned to his cabin where, with the help of his assistant and one of the girls, we consumed two bottles of white wine, one bottle of Georgian champagne, caviar, honey and crab-meat. Afanasyev lived in Leningrad, was 55 years old, and evidently well-paid. He lectured me about living in peace and showed why he meant it. One of his legs was five centimetres shorter than the other—from the defence of Leningrad. In addition, he had two steel plates in place of ribs—from the defence of Stalingrad. Although renamed Volgograd after the death of Stalin, Afanasyev used the old name, as did all veterans of that horrific campaign of 1942–43.

Nineteen days had now elapsed since making my measurements on Hayes Glacier, so I asked Somov and Kornilov, the leader of the station, whether I could go there again to see how far the glacier had moved. Yury Model agreed to come again and we returned to Molodezhnaya that evening armed with a fine set of measurements. On reaching the base we were revived with medicinal alcohol by courtesy of the station doctor Oleg Zhukov. I was later able to calculate that the centre of the glacier had moved 42 metres since our first observations—a speed equivalent to 800 metres per year. This, I knew, was fast compared with most Antarctic glaciers.

Ob finally sailed from Molodezhnaya on 12 March and headed west on the last leg of our voyage. But first the ship moved to a position where, nosing up against an icefoot, we could fill the ship's fresh water tanks by pumping from a lake 300 metres inland.

Ob at Molodezhnaya station

61

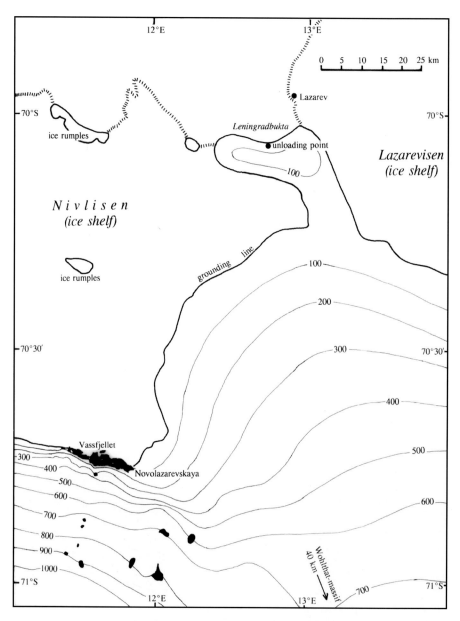

The approaches to Novolazarevskaya

After four days with very little sea ice in sight, we steamed through longitude 16° east, where I began this narrative and where Captain Bellingshausen saw distant mountains 144 years earlier. After rounding a big glacier tongue we turned south and approached our destination in longitude 13°E. A few kilometres away on the port side we spotted a derelict Il-12 aircraft at the abandoned Lazarev station. Lazarev had been occupied for two years (1959–1960), but because of excessive snow accumulation that buried the buildings, it was decided to move it inland to the nearest place where buildings could be constructed on rock. This was accomplished during the 1960–61[2] summer season, and the new station became known as Novolazarevskaya (new Lazarev).

Ahead of the ship we spotted a group of men on a small coastal ice rise. Beside them were two big artillery tractors, one farm tractor, many sledges and two Antonov-6 biplanes. This was the unloading point for Novolazarevskaya. The tractors were here to carry everything over the last 90 km to the station.

Moored to a four-metre high ice wall I saw, among a crowd of men, three of our own wintering team who had flown from Molodezhnaya to speed the handover from the outgoing crew.

The next two days were overcast and windy, but we spent the time unloading. Finally, at midnight, all was ready. Somov, the Captain and Viktor Koshevoy came ashore to exchange fond farewells and good wishes for the winter. The Captain and First Mate gave me a fine inscribed picture book of the USSR. Then, by the light of searchlights and signal flares, we freed *Ob*'s six hawsers from their deadmen, and she backed out into a sheet of new ice. A small cheering group on deck shouted *Do svidaniya* (goodbye) as rockets were launched from the bridge.

Six of us remained ashore. Together with the eight of our team at Novolazarevskaya, we were to live together in close quarters for 12 months, come what may. By this time I had become well acquainted with my colleagues and had no qualms but, as *Ob* vanished into the mist, the finality of the moment was brought home to each of us.

The stars shone brightly and a cold wind cut through our clothing. It was time for bed, and I wondered how we would spend the night. Our 'hotel' was a sledge with a caboose built on it. There were three narrow bunks on each of two walls. I was given a bottom bunk with a sleeping-bag on it. An anthracite stove kept us warm and meals were cooked on propane burners. We were so voracious for food after the long hours of rolling fuel drums that we opened some tins and laced our coffee with thick, sweetened condensed milk before collapsing on the bunks. The caboose was uninsulated, so that there was

Overnight in the caboose en route to Novolazarevskaya.
Left to right: Vasily Boriskin, the author, Aleksey Semochkin, Nikolay Yeremin

Nikolay Yeremin, leader of Novolazarevskaya station

an extreme temperature gradient between the floor and the roof. I slept in my bag, the man above slept on his bag, and the top man was sweating in his underwear.

The next morning it was blowing and snowing, so we slept and chatted. Some fine clear weather followed, and we spent the morning stacking and lashing cargo on two 20-tonne sledges. One of the sledges held provisions, the other general cargo. Cabooses on a pair of 10-tonne sledges held perishables. Except for a small space round the stove, each was filled to the ceiling with foodstuffs that had to be kept from freezing: sacks of cabbage, potatoes, cheese, cases of bottled jam, pickles and fruit; even cases of Georgian mineral water which no Russian, it seemed, will be without. The idea of delivering to an Antarctic station large quantities of food which must not freeze was itself unusual; most expeditions simply let their potatoes freeze and bring other perishables in tins, where they can freeze without damage.

The doctor, Vasily Boriskin, was appointed Chief Stoker and I was his assistant. Night and day we had to ensure that none of the stoves burned out. Another job was akin to that of the railway wheel-tapper, but here the object was to hammer in track bolts that were threatening to fall out and bring the tractor to a halt.

Tractors on the way from the coast to Novolazarevskaya. The sledges carry everything except the station fuel supply

65

Doctor Vasily Boriskin

Aleksey (Liosha) Semochkin

When finally we set off for Novolazarevskaya, our two Tyagach tractors and one smaller tractor were hauling every item—except fuel—required to maintain 14 men in the Antarctic for a full year. For one accustomed to seeing relays of tractors crawling back and forth between ship and shore, these were colossal loads. I was invited to ride in the cab of one of the big tractors with Nikolay Yeremin, our leader, and Aleksey Semochkin, a mechanic.

The trail led uphill for a time until the slope levelled off and then inclined down. It was midnight and the sun had just dipped below the horizon far inland, silhouetting pyramids of rock and illuminating lenticular clouds poised on standing waves high above the mountains. I did not need a map to identify what I was seeing. The biggest block was Wohlthat-massif, 160 km from where we were standing. Simply to cast eyes on this scene was for me a thrilling moment. Fourteen years earlier I had been a member of the Norwegian-British-Swedish expedition of 1949–52, one of whose objectives had been to reach and study Wohlthat-massif. As I related in an earlier book, we never made it.[3] Now at least I had seen the mountain. So near yet so far— it was tantalizing.

On reaching the foot of the ice rise, I realized that we were moving onto the flat surface of a floating ice shelf. Grinding on for a

Our first view of Wohlthat-massif (left), the 'unattainable' mountain range 160 km inland

further 45 km we stopped at dusk, and made radio contact with *Ob* and Novolazarevskaya.

After a good night's sleep it was decided to leave the farm tractor here because the surface had become too rough in relation to the short tracks. Its load was transferred to the artillery tractors, one of which now set out to haul about 60 tonnes, a truly fabulous load.

Ahead was a long and low-lying nunatak rising not much above the level of the ice shelf. It had first been seen from the air in 1939 by a secret German expedition intending to claim sovereignty over this area.[4] The Germans called it Schirmacherseenplatte after Richardheinrich Schirmacher, pilot of one of the expedition's flying boats. Russians call it Oazis Schirmakhera, Norwegians call it Vassfjellet, and Americans call it Schirmacher Hills. The Norwegians refer to the area as Schirmacheroasen (oasis). I cannot think of a better example of

Vassfjellet from the north. The ice shelf in the foreground is riven by melt streams. The arrow points to Novolazarevskaya station

place-name confusion on any continent; but, without a common language, such is the nature of Antarctic place-name decision-making—or the lack of it. Somewhere on the nunatak, I was told, Novolazarevskaya nestled in a hollow, but we would not see it until we were very close.

The surface now became ice-hard and there were melt streams blocking our path. Some of the stream channels we drove across were two metres wide and a metre deep, so the tractors struggled at walking pace while the sledges skidded wildly from side to side. Twice the towing cables parted and we had to replace them. The second artillery tractor was being driven by Vadim Prokopiev, our tractor mechanic, with Mojmír Konečný and the doctor as passengers. Whenever Prokopiev's tractor was brought to a halt—as many times it was—he would fire a signal flare over our heads as a cry for help. We had to unhitch our load, return and place our tractor ahead of his train, connect them together and, with a mighty jerk, move forward in tandem. Laboriously, we climbed from the ice shelf back onto the inland ice.

Nearing our destination, we crossed a medial moraine, a long line of boulders slowly being carried along by the ice from some distant rock outcrop beyond our horizon. It was now dark, and ahead of us, I spotted four white and five red lights. 'Our city!' said Yeremin. First

Our tractors had to cross melt streams like this. Sometimes they got stuck and had to be pulled out

69

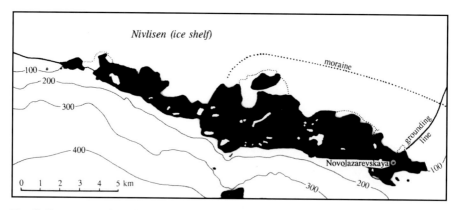

Vassfjellet, our oasis. The areas along the shore within fine dotted lines are tidal sea lakes. The medial moraine, at first parallel with the shore, curves southward, indicating that this part of the ice shelf is moving towards the land. Melting at the shoreline balances the southward flow

to greet us was Robert Pyzhov, the aerologist, and after we had piled out of our noisy machines, he showed me to my quarters in a four-room rectangular hut. It was the geophysical laboratory and living quarters, set 100 metres apart from the other four main buildings to reduce any disturbance to very sensitive magnetic instruments. Tolya and I were to share a 13-square-metre room. Each of us had a comfortable spring bed, desk, chair, cupboard and bookshelves. Two windows were each glazed with four panes of glass separated by air gaps to keep out the cold. Ventilation was provided by a hole drilled through the wall; in storms it could be plugged with a tampion. Between us we had a short-wave radio, ostensibly to receive time signals, a calculating machine, a typewriter and a telephone to the other buildings. A toilet in the entrance lobby consisted of a hole in the floor with half an empty fuel drum beneath. There was a boardwalk to the main buildings. I realized that before the year was out, each of us would walk over it more than 1000 times in each direction to take meals in the dining-room.

Yeremin presided over the Pentagon, a 9 × 8-metre hut devoted to meteorology and the radio station. His one privilege was to have a room of his own. Forty metres from the Pentagon was the aerology and medicine hut. Beyond that was the cooking/dining hut, and beyond that the power house and workshop. The separation was deliberate, based on the premise that a fire in one building should not spread to another. The disastrous fire at Mirny in 1960 had left an indelible mark on those who had designed subsequent stations. Novolazarevskaya had first been opened in 1961.

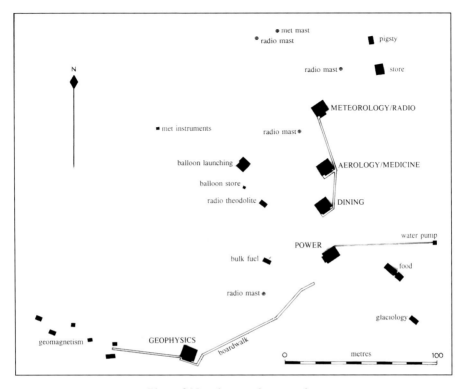

Plan of Novolazarevskaya station

The dining-room was the social centre of the community. It was 9 metres long and 4.5 metres wide. One long table accommodated all of us together. At one end of the room were library shelves and a film projector, at the other end a bust of Lenin and *Dobro pozhalovat* (welcome) scrawled on a long red banner. A portrait of Nikita Khrushchev hung on the long outer wall. Just inside the three windows, dwarf tomatoes were grown in window boxes. A doorway off the big room opened into the kitchen and a ready-use food store.

The main buildings were of identical size and construction. Consisting of prefabricated panels joined together, they had been specially made for the Antarctic at a factory in Kharkov. The panels were heavily insulated and some had built-in window frames. There were several smaller buildings: a radiosonde balloon-launching hut, a hut with a radio theodolite to track the balloons, an equipment store, a food store and a glaciology lab which I would have all to myself. I found a disused wooden hut floored with manure and sawdust. Evidently it was the former pigsty. So here there would be no fresh pork for our feast days.

71

The library included the collected works of Shakespeare in eight volumes. A popular evening pastime was dominoes

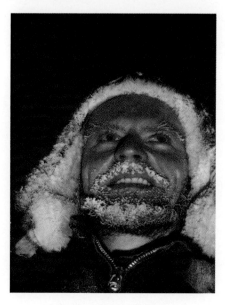

Anatoly (Tolya) Norman

The new arrivals were invited to enjoy a glorious hot splash-bath in the power-station hut. Then, greeted by all hands, we were faced with a magnificent midnight feast. Finally our little band was together in one place. My first impressions were all good. Over the past three months we had each sized up our colleagues and now I sensed an air of optimism about the winter ahead. Indeed we had to get on, because each depended on the others for survival. In case of emergency, we would be sobered by the thought that our nearest neighbours were at a Belgian station 470 km to the east. To the west there was a South African station 540 km along the coast, and there was nobody between us and the South Pole more than 2000 km away. To the north there was nothing but ocean as far as Cape Town.

6

Our 'City'

The staff, their responsibilities, dates of birth and the names by which
we addressed one another (bold type) were:

Aleksey (**Liosha**) Aleksandrovich Semochkin, electrician (1924)
Anatoly (**Tolya**) Yustinevich Norman, seismology/earth currents
(22/10/37)
Arkady (**Arkasha**) Andreevich Maksimov, meteorology
(22/09/37)
Charles Swithinbank, glaciology (17/11/26)
Gherman (German) Vasilyevich Floridov, radio operator
(08/03/38)
Ivan Maksimovich Sharikov, cook (20/06/17)
Mojmír Konečný, geomagnetism (4/10/31)
Nikolay Nikolayevich Yeremin, station leader (17/12/31)
Pavel Andreevich Tsvetkov, diesel mechanic (1919)
Robert Nikolayevich Pyzhov, second-in-command, aerology
(16/02/34)
Vadim Yevgenevich Prokopiev, tractor mechanic (1935)
Vasily Vasilyevich Boriskin, physician (22/01/20)
Vsevolod (**Seva**) Ivanovich Ladygin, aerology (18/04/38)
Yury (**Yura**) Petrovich Vereshchagin, geomagnetism/aurora
(14/08/36)

By this stage we were on first name or nickname terms, although, for
those who had no nickname, my colleagues almost invariably added
the patronymic.

The next few days were spent unloading the sledges and distribut-
ing the cargo, not without mishap as Vadim inadvertently reversed his
tractor over three drums of fuel, spilling 600 litres of diesel into the
snow.

I was impressed by the physical fitness of my companions. They
were able to heave 200-kilogramme (kg) fuel barrels with a reckless

Vadim Prokopiev

abandon that left me gasping. Perhaps, I thought, the average physical fitness of a nation in the modern world is inversely proportional to the number of motor vehicles in that country. Here I saw the same willingness to take part in hard manual labour that I had seen at Mirny. Coercion was not needed.

In daylight it became clear that our little cluster of buildings was in a hollow surrounded by low brown hills. Close by was a pond used for water supply. Less than a kilometre away on the south side rose the steep slope of the inland ice sheet. At the same distance on the seaward side, our patch of rock was bounded by a 100-metre high cliff overlooking the ice shelf that we had driven over. From the station there were no grand vistas of distant mountains. The whole nunatak, I was told, was 18 km long in an east–west direction and 1–2 km wide. There were gently rolling hills and freshwater lakes, two of them almost 800 metres in length. An ideal environment for hiking, I concluded, if people could take some time off. No wonder it was called an oasis.

Nikolay convened a meeting to discuss plans and the daily routine. I was surprised to find that he followed strict parliamentary procedure, opening with the election of a Chairman (diesel mechanic Pavel) and Secretary (radioman Gherman).[1] Controversial issues were put to the vote, and it became clear that Nikolay was intent on maintaining discipline by consent.

75

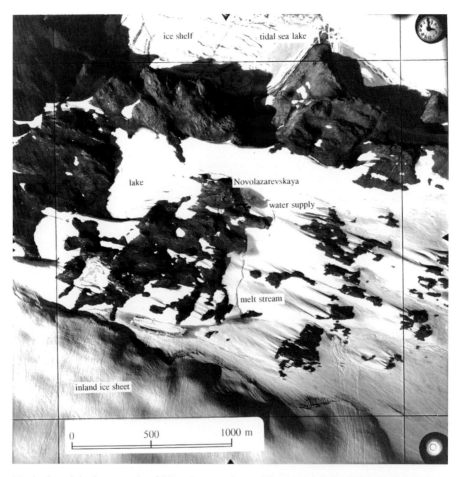

Vertical aerial photograph of Novolazarevskaya. The steeply sloping inland ice sheet (bottom) is only 2000 metres from the ice shelf and a tidal sea lake (top)

A second trip to the coast was being planned to collect diesel fuel for the power station. I asked if I could go along to make an elevation profile of the route using aneroid barometers. This was readily agreed because it meant one more pair of hands for cargo handling.

We departed with both artillery tractors and one empty sledge on 26 March in fine sunny weather. I rode with Liosha and Yura in the lead vehicle, and we forged ahead of the others. After crossing the moraine, Liosha stopped every 2 km for me to read three aneroid barometers and to drill in an aluminium stake. By measuring the height of the stakes on each visit I would get some idea of the rate

76

of snow accumulation—if there was any—or the rate of loss of ice from the surface. The stakes would also serve as trail markers.

By the time we stopped for the daily radio schedule at 2000, the air temperature had dropped to –28°C. We had covered 77 km and drilled in 36 stakes. Supper was a good deal better than on our first tractor trip. Now we had a choice of chicken, Australian ham, tuna fish, sardines, tomatoes, damsons, orange juice and fresh potatoes. Ivan had also supplied hamburgers.

Two hours driving the next day brought us to the coast. Then it took five hours of back-breaking labour to prepare the return loads. When again we headed south, one tractor was hauling 30 tonnes of fuel while the other had 11 tonnes of fuel plus a sledge piled high with lumber. In spite of crashing over rough terrain and having to re-lash the sledges every time their cargo shifted, we arrived home after another day's drive to be greeted by signal rockets, a big dinner and a glorious bath. Now everything we needed for the winter was in one place.

Nikolay had posted on the wall a rota for domestic duties. Taking turns, we had to sweep out the dining-room, do the washing up after meals and then stay on as night watchman. Apart from serving as fire watch, night duty involved regulating the voltage at the power station, topping up the oil, checking the coolant temperature and changing the

Ivan Sharikov in his sparsely furnished kitchen

paper on the 'crystal ball' (sunshine recorder). Although a chore, night duty only came round once every 14 days. The night watch ended when Ivan got up to cook breakfast.

Ivan was the oldest, tallest, baldest and humblest man at Novolazarevskaya, but one of the most likeable. He was born in Siberia and had lived there, he said, until he was 17. He was unable to get a higher education because his father was a *kulak* (a landowning farmer employing labour). After the revolutionary war (1917–23), kulaks were seen as exploiters of the peasantry and their families were treated harshly.

He had spent 13 years in the Arctic or Antarctic as a weather observer, and so loved the life that, when there were no further vacancies in that field, he signed on as cook. In the course of seven years in Franz Josef Land—five of them without a break—he married the senior station aerologist and she bore him a son. Childbirth was considered a domestic affair and was handled by the station doctor. Meanwhile both parents carried on with their jobs. On warm summer days, he said, the station crew sometimes bathed in the cold sea.

'So you saw no fighting in the war?' I asked.

'No, but we learned afterwards that there had been a secret German weather station on a nearby island.' Later, Ivan had wintered at 'North Pole-3' 'North Pole-5' and 'North Pole-7'. These were Soviet research stations built on drifting ice floes in the Arctic Ocean, ostensibly for weather observations but also—secretly—as listening posts for submarines. Some stations lasted for years.

When at home, Ivan and his family lived in a two-room 25-square-metre flat in an old building just off Nevsky Prospekt, the main street of Leningrad. To me that sounded comfortable enough until he admitted that three other families shared his kitchen and bathroom. In their private domain, they occupied less than 6.3 square metres per head (twice the area of a double bed), which at the time was the minimum living space to which every citizen was entitled. However, entitlement was one thing, reality another. Millions made do with less.

I had noticed that Russians tended to boast about their country's technical achievements, perhaps to compensate for their awareness of its shortcomings. For my part, I never glossed over the shortcomings of life in the West. Ivan and I became firm friends when he shed all pretensions and told me that he and his wife had spent their wedding night in the same room as his parents. 'We had to check that the folks were asleep before making love.' With a shrug he added, 'That's the way it was.'

He told me that he earned five times as much as the average Soviet worker. When I asked where the money had gone, Ivan replied with

78

a smile, 'High living, you know, we only live once.' However, he had saved something and was building a house in the countryside to use in retirement.

Ivan was somewhat lacking in culinary prowess, but did his best with what was available. He said that much of the food handed over by the 1963 wintering party was rotten, so he had to write off quantities of ham, sausage, meat loaf, chicken, duck and eight kinds of fish. Perhaps as a result of this, the most ubiquitous dish was *ragu* (ragout) consisting of stewed gristle with chips of bone, generally served with macaroni. Aside from the gristle, fat and bone, the amount of lean meat remaining could be held on a teaspoon. At almost every meal we had *borsch, shchi*, or fish soup with boiled potatoes. Then we helped ourselves to *compote* from a five-litre pot on the stove. Vigorous stirring before ladling out a cupful might capture a single segment of dried apple. The rest was a liquid the colour of weak tea.

One of my pet hates was fish-bun sandwiches. Pieces of slightly rehydrated dried codfish were separated with a cleaver and baked inside a bun. Chomping into the delicacy brought one's teeth sharply up against the bones, which then had to be separated by the tongue and, one after another, spat out. Fish soup brought the same problem.

Novolazarevskaya station. The meteorology/radio hut (informally known as the 'Pentagon') is behind our leader Nikolay Yeremin. The geophysics hut is at the far right behind the red balloon-launching shed

Ivan baked delicious black and white bread every day; there was *kasha* (porridge) for breakfast and unlimited butter and jam. There was also sometimes sauerkraut, tinned fish, black caviar and cheese. Tea and coffee were available at every meal. We never went hungry.

On request, Ivan also served as the community barber. His skill as coiffeur was never tested because he shaved most of our heads in the first few weeks. Tolya explained, 'Having no women here to admire my lovely hair, there's no point in having any; and it saves me the chore of combing.'

Mealtimes were at 0830, 1330 and 1930. Films were to be shown after dinner on five days a week. Our evenings were spent reading, playing chess or dominoes, or watching the films. There seemed to be a never-ending supply of 16-mm films, some about the revolution of 1917, the joys of life on collective farms, or holidays on the Black Sea coast. Perhaps best were the war films, packed with action and emotion. Although we saw films about heroes—or enemies of the state—there were never any about crime. Crime, I was told, will die out in socialist states because the wealth of the land is shared on a basis of equality. In a perverse way, American films were popular because in them there was no ideological barrier to portraying crime and violence.

The local equivalent of popcorn during films was a supply of ground nuts—monkey-nuts as we called them in my youth. We cracked each one between our teeth and scattered the husks over the table.

Saturday was bath day, when the bathroom next to the diesel generators was filled with steam and we would pile in to splash in basins of hot water. It was a social occasion involving much merriment and mutual back-scrubbing. 'Wet' bath days alternated with 'dry' bath days. On wet bath days we retired to the changing room to be given a glass of fruit drink laced with de-icing fluid.

Tolya and I shared the geophysical hut with Yura and Mojmír. Yura was a jovial, bearded 27-year-old physicist from Leningrad. He had been evacuated to Siberia with his family for $3\frac{1}{2}$ years during the war. He now lived with his physicist wife Ludmila and daughter Nina in a small flat with shared kitchen and bathroom. To reach their own room, he said, they had to go through his mother-in-law's room.

Every day at 1730 Mojmír and Yura would invite us into their room for coffee. The supply of coffee beans was unlimited, but the coarse grinder in the kitchen produced a rather insipid brew. Skilled with his hands, Mojmír rescued a high-speed hydraulic pump from parts of an old aircraft and converted the motor into a fine coffee

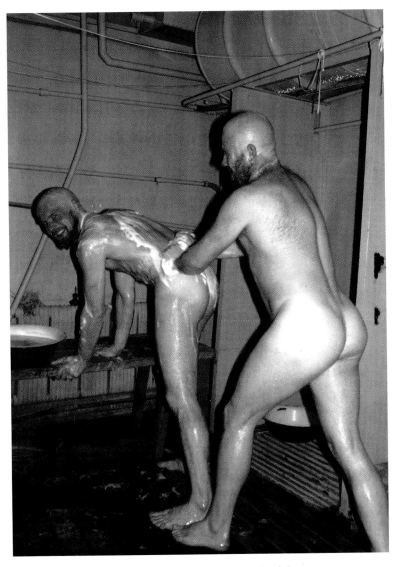

Mutual back-scrubbing on bath night

grinder. Our coffee tasted better than Ivan's, so sometimes we had a stream of visitors at that hour. Both Mojmír and Yura were pipe-smokers, so the air was filled with smoke.

I kept the remaining half-gallon flasks of Australian port wine under my bed to ensure that they never reached the height of a table. In this way I was able to spin out my riches for months of convivial

81

sessions after the coffee hour. There were other little social clubs in other buildings but, in those too, guests were made welcome.

Tolya and I generally retired to our quarters after the evening film and sometimes chatted for hours. Asked about his home, he said that his mother was Russian but his father was an Estonian doctor. Tolya was evacuated to Sverdlovsk in the Urals for the duration of the war, but his father stayed in Leningrad. After schooling in Tallinn, the capital of Estonia, he enrolled in Leningrad University to study physics, which led in due course to geophysics. He married at age 19 while still in college, a move I believe he regretted. Living in Tallinn, he and his wife Svetlana shared a one-room flat with another family. Svetlana worked as a construction engineer on the railways.

Tolya wanted to return to Novolazarevskaya for yet another winter to earn money to buy a car or a larger flat. A Moskvich could be bought for about 4500 roubles (£1800) or a Volga for 5500 (£2200), roughly the equivalent of a year's salary in the Antarctic.

Tolya earned 480 roubles (£190) per month in the Antarctic but only 140 (£56) a month at home. He said that his high salary in the Antarctic was really incentive pay, a concession to the first stage of Marxism-Leninism, after which people should have developed a social conscience 'like you', so that they give of their best irrespective of any reward.

I said, 'What do you mean by "like me"?'

He responded, 'Well, you have come to the Antarctic for 18 months without requiring any extra pay, which I would not have done. But that is the sort of thing that a social conscience should foster.'

Tolya wanted to continue in research, but told me that to be awarded a PhD one had to submit a dissertation on 'The principles of dialectic materialism'. When I asked him to translate, he said, 'Why socialism is better than capitalism.'

Every day I wrote my diary and together we listened to music. We each kept in touch with the outside world, he by listening to the news from Radio Moscow and I by tuning his radio to the BBC. By this time I was able to keep up with the Russian and he had no difficulty with the English. Often there was such a contrast between the Moscow and London versions of the same event that one of us would catch the other's eye and together we would roar with laughter. We seldom discussed which version was the more likely to be true.

We heard other angles on world affairs from the 'Voice of America' and 'Radio South Africa'. Hearing that Leon Uris's book *Exodus* contained much criticism of the British government, with a sly grin Tolya asked me where it was published. Evidently he assumed that because of its content it must have been published abroad and banned in the UK.

Tolya had heard of a place in London called Hyde Park Corner where any man could stand up and address a crowd without fear of prosecution, even if he spoke about the iniquities of the British government and the evils of capitalism. I confirmed the truth of his story but added that, if the man chose a different street corner, he would not be arrested there either. This paradox left Tolya quite perplexed.

Getting to know each other better, we sometimes discussed history and politics. He had hair-raising tales to tell about the great purges of the 1930s. Millions of people felt threatened by the secret police, and denouncing one's colleagues on concocted evidence made it less likely that the denouncer, having demonstrated his loyalty to Stalin, would himself be arrested. One way to settle a personal grudge was to drop a note in a mailbox reporting that you had overheard a colleague criticizing Stalin. The culprit was named but it was not necessary to sign the denunciation. The named person would disappear and might never be seen again. Tolya knew that Stalin had killed more Russians than Hitler.

He had no illusions about an imminent socialist paradise, though he believed that his countrymen were emerging from a long tunnel of repression into something closer to freedom. My own judgement was that they had spotted a point of light at the far end of that tunnel, but there was a long way to go before they could emerge into the daylight.

In discussing the meaning of democracy, I said that the freedom to travel wherever and whenever one wanted, without asking anyone's permission, was to me an essential ingredient. I asked if he resented not being allowed to emigrate or travel abroad. 'Naturally I would like that freedom,' he replied, 'but, for the present, our country needs to catch up with the West, so we cannot afford to lose people who have been educated at the expense of the state.' For now he accepted the restriction, but 'in time it will pass.'

On 27 March, Tolya's seismographs recorded a massive event somewhere in the northern hemisphere, and afterwards we heard that the city of Anchorage in Alaska had been devastated by an earthquake. More than 130 people lost their lives and the damage was estimated at $200 million.

On bad weather days when I could not work outside, I often found myself in the doctor's room yarning away the hours. One of the potential problems of a physician looking after 14 healthy men was that there was very little work to do. However, Vasily knew that in Antarctica one had to be prepared for any kind of emergency.

I told him that I had been on an expedition where the doctor had to take out a man's eye.[2] He capped that by relating how in 1961 L.I. Rogozov, the doctor at Novolazarevskaya, had taken out his own appendix with the help of a mechanic and a meteorologist. It was a harrowing story. At the time, a blizzard was raging and it was impossible to get medical help from any other station. 'The patient' recognized in himself the symptoms of peritonitis. He prepared syringes and instructed his assistants that, if he lost consciousness, they were to use the drugs and administer artificial respiration. Then he propped himself in a semi-reclining position, injected Novocaine, and made the incision. Throughout the operation, one of the assistants had to kneel holding a mirror so that Rogozov could see what he was doing. The doctor developed vertigo after 30–40 minutes and had to pause for rests.

After resection of the severely diseased vermiform appendix (a 2 × 2 cm perforation was found at its base), antibiotics were introduced into the peritoneal cavity, and the wound was tightly sutured.[3]

The operation took two hours and the patient made a complete recovery. Vasily then told me that, in 1960, three southbound expedition members contracted a venereal disease on a visit to Cape Town. Since the appropriate drugs for treatment were not on board, the men had to work for several months in the Antarctic before being sent home in the ship. As a form of punishment, their wives were told why they were not spending the winter in the Antarctic as planned.

I found Vasily to be more mature than any of the other men and he never minced words. Born in 1919, he came from peasant stock living near Tula (200 km south of Moscow) and went to school barefoot because his parents could not afford shoes. His birth certificate was destroyed by fire during the Civil War, so he lied about his age in order to enter medical school. He had reason to be grateful to the Party and the system because, despite his humble origins, he had become a doctor, graduating entirely at the expense of the state. 'Could that happen in your country?' he asked.

His parents, like most peasants, were against the collectivization of farms. But he remembered the excitement in his village, in about 1930, when the first tractor appeared. 'People gathered from miles around to look at it.' Vasily's father was now a storekeeper, his mother a charwoman, his sister a ticket-collector.

The war years saw him in the thick of it. He was an army doctor at the battle of Stalingrad during the worst period in 1942, when the

German army was attacking from the north. 'A vehicle I was travelling in at night was hit by a shell and overturned; I was severely wounded.' He returned to the battlefront as an Air Force doctor in White Russia (Belarus), chasing the German army into Poland. Finally, in 1945, he fought westwards from Leningrad through the Baltic states.

Vasily's earlier polar work had included a tour of duty on the North Pole-6 drifting station in the Arctic. As a research physiologist he was paid 450 roubles (£180) per month at home but 750 roubles (£300) in the Antarctic. With his Antarctic earnings he had bought a Volga car. He now lived in Leningrad in a three-room flat with his wife Nadezhda, their two sons, and his mother. Nadezhda, a general practitioner, was paid only 80 (£32) roubles per month. The family's charwoman, he said, was paid 35 roubles (£14).

I asked why general practitioners were paid less than many a factory worker or farm-hand. 'Well,' he said, 'they had ten years of training at the expense of the state, during which time they were unproductive. By being low-paid they are reimbursing the state. That's fair, isn't it?'

At Novolazarevskaya, Vasily was studying changes in the central nervous system, mental acuity and physical fitness, particularly in relation to the isolation and winter darkness. Once a month we were

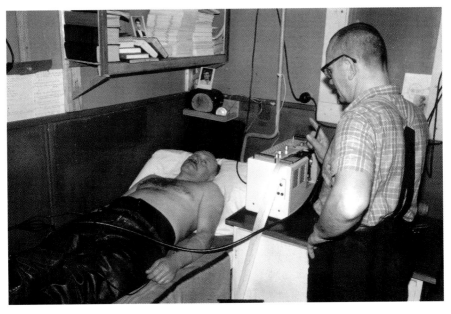

Vasily monitoring Ivan with electrocardiograph

85

asked to lie on his couch and be connected to an electrocardiograph. Then he measured our blood pressure and tested our sight, night vision, hearing, nerve sensitivity and reaction times. Next he took blood and urine samples to carry home for biochemical studies. He was convinced that while the Antarctic climate itself had no deleterious effects, our isolation led to some loss of mental acuity. Together with earlier studies he had made at Arctic stations, he was hoping to write up his findings for a doctoral dissertation.

Vasily had a deep interest in politics. One day I found him reading *Principles of Scientific Atheism.* Another time I found him poring over *Spravochnik Agitatora*, which translates as the 'Agitator's reference book', though in reality it was a communist propagandist's handbook. Later, I borrowed the book. On the face of it, the pages were filled with convincing arguments on the merits of communism and the evils of capitalism. Responses were offered for almost every conceivable question or argument that might be put forward by sceptics. Graphs presenting various criteria of industrial productivity for both the USSR and the US showed steady or slowly rising indices for the US against steeply rising indices for the USSR. While most of the Soviet indices were below those of the US, they invariably overtook them when projected a few years ahead. Cynically, I wondered whether the crossing point of the curves was shifted to the right in each new edition to reflect the continuing gap between aspiration and achievement. When I had finished the book, however, I felt that, if ever I chose to espouse communist ideology, I could win any debate with a Western audience and exhaust them to boot. The 'evidence' was there in the graphs. It was a dangerous book, I concluded, for anyone naïve enough to accept what it sought to prove.

Vasily told me that he himself, Nikolay, Robert and Pavel were full members of the Communist Party; Vadim was a candidate member; while Seva, Ivan, Arkasha and Tolya were members of *Komsomol*, the Young Communist League.

April 1st is as much All Fool's Day in Russia as it is in England. There were a number of leg-pulling escapades such as reporting that Leningrad was on fire or our ice shelf had drifted out to sea. All were taken in good humour.

7

Excursion

It was becoming clear to me that nobody else's job required leaving the immediate vicinity of the station buildings. I had never encountered this on earlier expeditions and nobody had briefed me about it. In my work I needed to travel at least 10 km away, but safety precautions meant that nobody was permitted to leave the station alone. I pleaded with Nikolay but he insisted that no exception could be made to the rule. I could travel if I found someone to accompany me; but that would not be easy. Needing good weather, any glaciologist starts at a disadvantage, so adding this extra constraint meant that my work might be much less productive than the work of my colleagues. I was depressed and my friends saw it.

I had noted a low knoll about a kilometre from the station that would be ideal for surveying ice-movement stakes a considerable distance away. My heart had been set on studying the deformation of the ice sheet across the the so-called 'grounding line', where the inland ice sheet begins to float on the sea. From the knoll I could command a view of the best areas, while still being within sight of the station.

Awaiting a day when someone was free to help, I prepared 90 new stakes by sawing lengths of aluminium tube. These had been brought to the station by an earlier wintering glaciologist, who never found time to use them. Then, with time to spare, I helped Mojmír to build a new shed for his instruments.

There came a day when Nikolay agreed to accompany me to reconnoitre the area. We found a second potential survey station and erected a theodolite tripod on it. Now I could measure angles to each stake from this and the little peak I had earlier identified. By measuring the distance between the points, I could determine the exact position of each stake by simple trigonometry. A resurvey some months later should, with luck, give accurate values of the rate of ice movement.

The next day, 6 April, was my first day of real work. Nikolay, Liosha and I drove off in one of the artillery tractors with 16 empty fuel drums and all my new stakes. Climbing up the ice sheet behind the station, we fixed 13 drums at 1 kilometre intervals, so that each of them was visible from both survey stations. But crossing melt streams made for a bumpy ride because some were now hidden under snow.

Four days later I was allowed one last excursion. Nikolay, Pavel, Seva and I loaded up with 21 empty fuel drums, then followed the tracks to seaward over very rough terrain and melt streams. On the return, we laid 12 drums in a straight line and the other six in a line at right angles. In the hurry to beat the setting sun, at one point the tractor became stuck astride a wide stream and was unable to move forward or backward. It took minutes of violently turning and jerking to escape. On arriving back at base just as the last twilight left us, Nikolay made clear that the tractor needed an overhaul, so this was the last excursion of the season.

There followed several days of bad weather. Accosting Liosha one day, I asked him to explain how the huts were heated. Without hesitation he launched into the basics: 'Well, we get 10 kilocalories from each gram of diesel fuel, right? 38% is lost in the exhaust, 6% is lost in friction and heating the oil, 25% is carried away by the cooling fluid, and 31% remains to drive the generator.'

I was impressed that a humble electrician was able to reel off figures like this. He went on to explain that two of the huts, the bathroom and the water pipes from the pond were heated entirely by waste heat from the cooling fluid. The Pentagon and the geophysics building were heated by electric immersion heaters. A single 24 kilowatt generator handled the whole electrical load.

Liosha was a colourful character whose initial training had been as an aircraft mechanic and, in that capacity, he had served throughout the war. Afterwards he worked at the North Pole-5 drifting station. Then he spent a year at North Pole-6 with Nikolay, Ivan and Vasily, so these four at least had known each other for some time. Liosha had wintered at Vostok in 1959 and also during the first winter at Novolazarevskaya in 1961. Although unmarried, he had built his own house near Leningrad and owned a car. He shared the house with his parents and sister. Asked about the ownership of private property, he said that anyone could legally own 'a castle' as long as they paid for it out of legitimate earnings.

Pavel, the 44-year-old diesel mechanic, was a giant of a man weighing 94 kg, which as it happened was twice the weight of his diminutive assistant Vadim. He had wintered at Mirny in 1958 and at Vostok in 1961. One of his three sons was wintering 1500 km to the east of us at Molodezhnaya. Pavel's domain was the power station, though he had been trained as a metalworker and instrument maker. He oversaw our three diesel generators: one in use, one on standby, and the third being overhauled. It was a shock to a Westerner to find that there were almost no spare parts. However, the mechanics, well-trained in workshop practice, could make almost anything. Their pride and joy was a giant East German lathe that had travelled east as part of war reparations.

Breakdowns of vehicles were not uncommon, and Pavel and his co-workers calmly launched into repairing them. Tongue-in-cheek, they recited the official mantra: 'Soviet technology is the best in the world!' This invariably gave rise to snickers all round.

Pavel had cut his teeth as a Red Army driver in the 'Great Patriotic War', chasing the front line through Romania, Poland, Czechoslovakia, Poland, Germany and Austria. During the siege of Leningrad (1941–44) he was driving the winter supply route over Lake Ladoga.

With competence born of necessity, he and his colleagues kept the Novolazarevskaya power station running for 24 hours a day through-out the year. The total time lost to breakdowns was just 10 minutes in 365 days—a remarkable achievement.

Pavel's ingenuity was unbounded. On dismantling one of the diesels he discovered that the cooling-fluid impeller was broken. It was a bronze casting with many curved blades and there was no way to repair it. With typical sang-froid Pavel fashioned a new and identical impeller out of a solid block of brass. It was so perfectly finished and balanced that I would have assumed it came from the factory.

One day Pavel bet his long golden hair against half of Vasily's hair that Vasily could not beat him at table tennis. Pavel lost the bet and later appeared—bald-headed. On another occasion some practical jok-ers put a 200-kg anvil under Pavel's pillow; he only discovered it when he lay down. Thus, from time to time, did my comrades relieve the monotony of the winter night.

Vadim, Pavel's assistant, was the smallest of my colleagues (he weighed 47 kg). His short stature and youthful complexion belied his 29 years. A native of Leningrad, he left school at 15 but later had years of part-time training. His father was Dean of the Physical Education Faculty at Moscow State University, while his mother had been a surgeon during the war but now specialized in internal medi-cine at a Leningrad hospital.

Vadim was delightful company at work or play. He had been 'on wheels', meaning away from home, for the last 20 years. He served in Kazakhstan for six years as a tractor driver/mechanic on a Komsomol *Sovkhoz* (state farm), ploughing up virgin steppe to grow grain. His first polar work was as a member of an expedition to the

Vadim Prokopiev repairing a tractor

New Siberian Islands, where he spent eight months in 1960. Since then he had wintered at Mirny in 1962. He was superbly skilled as a mechanic, and tough to boot—I once found him repairing a tractor at night, in the open, at a temperature of −20°C. Grinning, he quipped: 'You know, Charles, Soviet technology is the best in the world!'

As projectionist for our films, Vadim was the butt of some teasing because he was accident-prone. Once he plugged the loudspeaker leads into a 220-volt socket, with the result that smoke instead of music came out. Another time he started the projector without a take-up spool, and in the darkness failed to notice until there was a tangled heap of film on the floor. But he was unfailingly cheerful and, many times I was impressed by his ability to repair baulky machinery under almost any conditions.

Vadim had *Nina*, the name of his first love, tattooed on his left hand, which displeased his wife Maria, a chemical engineer working in a research institute. They lived in Leningrad with their five-year-old daughter. He asked me to send him a copy of Boris Pasternak's *Doctor Zhivago*, which was banned in the Soviet Union.

In their spare time during the winter, Pavel and Vadim made works of art, among other things a curved brass mounting such as would support a globe. Instead of a globe, however, they fitted into it an emperor-penguin egg. Later, the whole evocative ornament was pre-

Mojmír Konečný

sented to me for my birthday, and I treasure it. During the course of
the year, each of us was presented with an artistic memento of some
kind.

The geophysicists Tolya, Mojmír and Yura had to make observations and check their recording instruments every few hours. Tolya
had an alarm bell in our room, which went off when there was an
earthquake of more than a certain magnitude. He recorded many an
earthquake from distant parts of the world, but he was also studying
the extent to which the Antarctic continent itself was seismically
active. He had found 'icequakes', which he interpreted as being
caused by icebergs calving from one of the ice shelves. His other
research programme was in 'earth currents', measuring the natural
electrical field of the earth between electrodes set some distance apart.

Mojmír was studying geomagnetism by making continuous records
of short-period fluctuations caused by solar activity and magnetic
storms. Another study entailed the recording of atmospheric and exos-
pheric noise. In blizzards, static electricity generated by the friction of
snow against the aerials was conducted into the hut through Mojmír's
aerials, giving a spectacular high-voltage stream of sparks jumping a
gap to the earth terminal.

I admired the care with which Mojmír and also his colleagues
frequently calibrated their instruments to ensure that accurate

Tolya at work

Mojmír with La Cour magnetometers

Yury Vereshchagin with quartz horizontal magnetometer

Everyday lunch

comparisons could be made between their results and observations from other stations. Yura's task was complimentary to Mojmír's. He made daily precise ('absolute') measurements of the magnetic field of the Earth and its fluctuations. He had to go out in all weathers to isolated huts housing ultra-sensitive magnetometers. Only copper nails had been used in the construction of these 'non-magnetic' huts, in order to escape from local magnetic fields induced by ferrous metals. Yura's other job was to study the aurora in relation to other geophysical phenomena. An 'all-sky' camera with a fish-eye lens continuously photographed the heavens during the dark period.

At lunch one day Tolya bet his beard that Pavel could not hammer in a 10-centimetre copper nail at the first attempt without bending it. They both disappeared to the workshop to settle the matter. Half an hour later Tolya appeared without a beard.

Nikita Khrushchev's birthday was on the 17th April and Seva's on the 18th. Nobody wanted two parties in a row, so we postponed Khrushchev's until the 18th. During a run of bad weather before and after this celebration, I spent my time reading reports of earlier Soviet expeditions, copying maps, poring over aerial photographs and used a sewing-machine to make red flags for the stakes. There was much to study, so I was never idle.

Lenin's birthday was 22 April. There was no official celebration but

A painting to inspire the cook. It didn't

94

Vasily, as senior party member, gave a half-hour lecture about Lenin's life and its historical significance. It was well and sincerely delivered. Afterwards, I entertained the geophysicists with a glass of port to mark the occasion.

Tolya heard on the radio that 23 April was William Shakespeare's 400th birthday. On mentioning this to Nikolay, he drew my attention to the complete works of Shakespeare in our library. There was a handsomely bound eight-volume set (in Russian). There were 15 books by Lenin, including *On the Building of the Party* and *On Communist Morals*, and a number about him. We had *Dialectics of Nature* by Friedrich Engels, *Selected Works* of Karl Marx, *Issues of Leninism* by Josef Stalin, *Communism, Peace and the Happiness of the People* by Nikita Khrushchev, *The Present International Situation and the Foreign Policy of our Country* by Cho En Lai and *Speeches 1961–63* by Fidel Castro. Then there was *Textbook of Political Economy*, *Fundamentals of Communist Training*, *Reference Book of the Party Worker* and *Contemporary International Problems*. In total, our political literature spanned more than two metres of bookshelf. 'Nothing,' my diary notes, 'is left to the imagination.'

There were also translations into Russian of works by Charles Dickens, Mark Twain, John Galsworthy (15 volumes), Jack London, Jules Verne, Anatole France, Nikolay Gogol, Stendhal (15 volumes), Thomas Mann (10 volumes) and Somerset Maugham. Drawing my attention to the packed bookshelves, Nikolay said, 'There, you see, we have a wide variety of foreign literature as well as Russian.' Later I realized that the Western literature in the library was largely selected, or at least approved, because the chosen authors wrote of the class distinctions that were held to be inherent in capitalist society.

The only English language book in the library was *Our Bessie* by Rosa Carey, published in New York around 1890. I had brought my own books and, as I finished each one, I would pass it on to anyone keen to read English. Seva the aerologist was the keenest reader.

I worked outside whenever the weather allowed. As the days passed it became clear that much of my survey work would be in the winter darkness, so I made an internal lighting system for the theodolite to be able to read off angles even at night. Of course I had to be able to see the stakes, but there would generally be enough twilight for that; they stood out well against the white background.

One fine day Seva volunteered to come with me to the survey stations to write down angle measurements as I read them off the theodolite. Sitting still for hours on end, he was chilled to the bone. By the time we returned to base, he was showing symptoms of hypothermia. After recovering his composure with a cup of coffee, I

We wore our best suits for national holidays: 1 May, 7 October and 1 January.
This is 1 May—I know because the oranges ran out shortly afterwards

prompted him to speak to Nikolay about the absurdity of the rule that I must not work alone—even within sight of the station. Anyone could check on my well-being simply by looking out of a window. Reluctantly, at supper time the leader gave way.

Now my work would be possible. My first solo day was on 29 April; I spent three hours taking angles. Afterwards I had to dismantle one of the two theodolites to realign the scale-reading system. It was midnight when I finished.

The next day everyone joined in to clean up the station prior to the May Day celebration. It was not easy. In 1964 there was no sign of what, decades later, would come to be known as environmental awareness. The place was unsightly with rubbish scattered far and wide. Empty bottles were thrown from doors to smash on the rocks outside. To reduce the risk of injury, we all wore calf-length boots. Paper and boxes were incinerated—if they were caught before they blew away.

May 1st was 'International solidarity of labour day'. Had it not been too windy outside, there would have been a *demonstratsiya* (demonstration) with formal flag-hoisting ceremonies. As it was, the celebrations began at lunch after everyone had been given time to change into their best clothes. The festive lunch included ham, crab

A formal group photograph. Back row: Arkasha, Liosha, Gherman, Vadim;
Middle row: Seva, Vasily, Ivan, Pavel, Tolya; Front row: Mojmír, the author,
Nikolay, Robert and Yura

Ice shelf scenery on a weekend excursion

salad, smoked salmon, salmon and sturgeon caviar, apples and oranges, and plenty of champagne and brandy. 'The occasion,' I noted, 'seems to have lost its political significance, and is just a holiday.' A film was shown in the afternoon. Supper consisted of roast chicken, leftovers from lunch, and orange juice laced with de-icing fluid. This was followed by another film.

May 2nd was also a holiday. Brunch was served at 1100, accompanied by two bottles of brandy and two of vodka. Suitably fuelled, ten of us drove off to enjoy an *ekskursiya* (excursion) in one of our two GAZ machines, the only relatively small tracked vehicles that we had. We behaved like schoolboys on a holiday outing. With Nikolay driving, the GAZ lurched and bounced westwards along the edge of the inland ice and over the gently rolling hills, stopping here and there for us to take photographs of lakes or the moraine-filled ice cliffs towering above us. Four hours later we returned to Novolazarevskaya with the vehicle radiator boiling from over-exertion.

There was a film show in the afternoon. At supper time I suspended the microphone of my tape recorder over the dining table and recorded everything going on—often two or three conversations at once. Nobody seemed inhibited by this intrusion. There was more

On weekend excursions we felt like truants. This is the inland ice cliff at the southern margin of Vassfjellet

98

drinking, together with fish soup, rissoles and tinned pineapples. Another film was shown afterwards. By bedtime I felt that there was a lot to be said for days with an *ekskursiya*.

May 5th was Karl Marx's birthday but there was no celebration. Instead, the four of us from the geophysical hut went to chop ice from the nearest pond. We piled blocks of ice outside the hut, ready to be brought in when the melting tank was getting low. Together, we used about 70 litres of water a day, partly for photographic processing (all three seismographs and also the ionosphere sounder used photographic recording paper) and partly for domestic purposes.

Throughout May I was only able to do survey work on about one day in five. For the rest, my diary entries note: 'windy', 'very windy', 'a real blizzard', 'high wind with intermittent drifting', or 'windy and cold'. Cold meant something below −10°C, though there was considerable variation from one day to the next.

For manual labour in summer, most of us wore ordinary gardening gloves. For colder conditions, we used thick woollen mittens inside leather outers, and for very cold conditions I used reindeer-skin gloves on top of everything else. However, a heavy load of clothing inevitably makes one clumsy, and the very worst thing for handling a theodolite is to touch any part of it other than the thumb screws. Touching the tripod, even lightly, can throw the instrument off its delicate balance. Keeping the hands warm was only a problem after taking off my gloves to make adjustments. By the time the pain became unbearable and I returned to the gloves, recovery took an age because hands *and* gloves had cooled during the interval.

The critical factor for outdoor work was not so much temperature as wind. Even a light breeze carries away several times more body heat than still air. In a book I found a table of the so-called wind-chill factor, showing the cooling power of moving air. At an air temperature of −20°C, for example, a 20-knot wind makes the body feel as cold as in still air at −35°C.[1]

Although bare skin is the most vulnerable, most of the time I wore nothing on my face. A face mask can protect to some extent, but it soon becomes ice-bound with condensation from breathing. From then on, it can only be separated from skin or beard after thawing indoors.

Among other tasks, I spent many of the bad-weather days writing up unfinished parts of my earlier work with the US Antarctic Research Program so that they could be published on my return home.[2] At this time also, I was asked to teach English to anyone interested, so found myself in front of a class of seven pupils three times a week. Although most of them claimed to have studied English in school for some years, Tolya was the only one who could con-

The author teaching English

verse. While I could offer them genuine English pronunciation, I was hopeless at explaining the rules of grammar. Tolya, armed with a Russian-language English grammar book, saved the day by discoursing with great skill on the intricacies of my native tongue. I did have the benefit of a Soviet teacher's handbook. It was well written, but I was disconcerted to discover that many of the practice sentences bore an undisguised ideolological message. Examples were:

'Workers in capitalist countries have few books.'
'Have you worked on a collective farm this summer?'
'How many Komsomol members are there in your class?'
'The Communist Party surrounds children with love and care.'
'Will you go to the Pioneer Palace today?'

To balance these sentences I asked them to repeat: 'We listen to a lot of propaganda.' That brought a good laugh.

I could of course construct my own sentences, but there was no way to stop my pupils seeing the textbook examples. Progress was slow, but I succeeded in getting them to compose and speak their own sentences. One day Yura searched in my dictionary for a pithy English word to use as an insult. Finding the right word—or so he thought—he hurled at his friend Tolya, 'Comrade, you are a *dreg*!'

Though there were drop-outs, there were also four very hard-working students who waded through several of the novels that I had brought with me.

Tolya decided that all this was the next best thing to an Antarctic University. Later in the year he prepared some impressive-looking graduation certificates that were formally presented to the pupils in front of their assembled colleagues.

In mid-May there were a series of strong blizzards, which made walking on the causeway difficult if not dangerous. From time to time, we would end up prostrate on the rocks, saved from injury only by our heavy clothing. While the separation of our buildings could serve as a deterrent to moving from one to another, I myself found that the unavoidable doses of fresh air were stimulating. Plodding the 100-metre boardwalk to and from the geophysical building several times a day, occasionally in pitch darkness and hurricane-force winds, with driven ice crystals seeming to sandpaper the face, was actually stimulating. An advantage was that when there were stars, we could see them; when there were curtains of the aurora australis dancing across the sky, we could marvel at them; and when the temperature dropped to –40°C, we could thrill at the blast of warm air on opening the door of the hut.

According to the nautical almanac, the sun was supposed to set for the winter on 19 May but, two days later, we caught a refracted glimpse of it sliding along the northern horizon. Then there was darkness, though there was always some twilight around noon that allowed me a few hours of survey work if the wind permitted.

30 May. Today I read a whole chapter in Russian for the first time. I have been making myself read scientific reports for at least an hour a day, plus an hour of grammar when I can find no excuse for not doing it...

Most of us received 100-word letters from home by radio once a month and could reply with 100 words. My wife taped some of her messages and mailed them to Radio Moscow, where they were read out in special Antarctic bulletins with everyone else's letters. Characteristically, most letters in both directions were cheerful, if rather bland, evidently because nobody wanted to risk causing concern. Another factor that inhibited the sharing of intimate personal feelings was that our private letters were all too public.

I asked Nikolay whether we might try to set up a link with the British Antarctic Survey as an alternative route for my mail. 'What?'

he exclaimed, 'make contact with a foreign radio station without permission!' At this he silently drew a finger across his throat, indicating that such action would be frowned upon by his superiors. However, he did seek permission and, after an interval, it came. From then on, I had a good radio link and could sometimes chat with the operator in Port Stanley, though mostly by morse code. One day when Gherman let me loose on the morse key, I tapped out: 'Go easy on the abbreviations old man as our operator has very little English.' He came back: 'Tell Tovarishch Gherman sorry but I thought his English sounded perfect.' My colleague proudly pinned this note on the wall of the radio room.

We also established a link with Stonington Island where my counterpart, the Russian exchange scientist Garik Grikurov, was living on a British station. He faced language difficulties in sending home his own radio letters because the British radio operator could not cope with the morse code in Russian. So he sent Grikurov's messages to us in English. With my help, Gherman then translated them into Russian before sending them on to Moscow. The resultant gibberish became known as 'Charles's Chinese.' Strange as it may sound, I had a conversation with Grikurov in which I spoke Russian and he responded in English. We were, after all, both speaking the language that we had been using for the past six months. I asked what he thought of the British way of travelling in the Antarctic (dog-sledging) and he replied, 'Heroic'. He meant obsolete.

8

Winter

Gherman was the son of a lorry driver and the manageress of a small shop. His home in Petrokrepost had been overrun by the Germans and his father was killed in the fighting. An only child, he and his mother spent the war as refugees. He well remembered the bombing and shelling from when he was five years old. Trained as a radio technician at Leningrad Arctic College, he worked for two years at Druzhnaya (Friendship) station on Hayes Island in Franz Josef Land. He was married to Emma, a geophysicist who also worked in the Arctic and they had one son. Emma had now changed direction and was in the second year of a correspondence course in English arranged by the Foreign Languages Institute in Moscow. The family

Gherman in one of his two radio rooms

103

lived in a large room in a house of two apartments with a garden of fruit trees.

Gherman's main job at Novolazarevskaya involved contacting Mirny five times a day to transmit weather data and all other communications. Another job was to record satellite signals; he had tape-recorders tracking *Polyet-2*, *Elektron-2*, *Elektron-3*, *Elektron-4* and *Kosmos-35*. Gherman was responsible for piping tape-recorded background music to all the main buildings. I lent him some of my music tapes and borrowed his, until I discovered that Russian tapes constantly shed iron filings into the critical parts of a tape-recorder. Comparing the quality of Russian taped music with my own made clear that the term 'hi-fi' was more than just a Western advertising slogan.

It was 3 June before I could report the first results of the ice-movement survey. A point on the inland ice sheet (resting on rock) was moving at the rate of 13 metres per year, and a point on the floating ice shelf was moving 22 metres per year. These speeds contrasted with speeds of up to 800 metres that I had measured two years earlier on the other side of the continent.

On 6 June it was 20 years since D-day, the day in 1944 when the Allied armies invaded France. At dinner that night Vasily, with no malice intended, proposed a toast to 'The day the Allies joined the war against German Fascism.' In the interests of harmony, I did not remind him that Britain declared war on Germany two years before his country did the same. This was one of many occasions on which perception mattered more than history.

> 8 June. Very high wind, a steady hurricane, force 12 [70 knots], gusting higher. Almost reduced to hands and knees on the causeway, and several times blown off it. All the huts are vibrating, and the galvanized iron sheets on the roof are lifting and banging.

The highest gust speed we recorded was 101 knots. It carried away a 25-metre section of the causeway and smashed the boards to matchsticks to bounce over the rocks.

On 21 June, Midwinter's Day, it was still possible to read a newspaper out of doors for about two hours, the sun being only four degrees below the horizon at noon. Our celebrations were muted and nobody dressed up. There was no vodka with dinner, only some de-icing fluid. Nikolay read out telegrams of greeting from other Antarctic stations: Byrd, McMurdo, Scott, Mawson, Davis, Wilkes, Mirny, Molodezhnaya and Vostok. Also one from President Lyndon B. Johnson of the United States.

18 July. Celebration in the evening for the return of the sun, which nobody saw as it was obscured by clouds. ... I hope it is the last time the sun rises in my life due north or due south. We had the usual feast fare. ... Then Cary Grant and Audrey Hepburn in 'Roman Holiday', with Russian voices...

I saw the sun for the first time on 22 July, half of it, sliding along the northern horizon. That same evening on my way home from teaching English, I was standing in awe of a particularly starry sky when I caught sight of a lone star moving across the heavens. I ran into the hut yelling 'Tolya, Sputnik!' Bursting out of the door, we followed it across the zenith and took bearings on its orbit: it was tracking 10° west of true north. On telling our colleagues what we had seen, all 14 of us went outside to marvel at it on its next pass. This, we knew, must be the first polar-orbiting satellite. It was also the first new artefact to come into our lives. Years later I learned that it was the American *Nimbus*, the first satellite launched by any country into a polar orbit.[1]

The next day we saw the satellite again as it sailed past the Southern Cross. We timed it, finding that it reappeared every 109 minutes. Mojmír and I both photographed its passage by setting 10-second time exposures.

Although there had been many a blizzard, very little snow had settled on the ground before early August. But now snowdrifts built a tail behind each of the buildings, and we had to keep a shovel at the ready to ensure that doorways never became blocked. None of the windows was designed to be opened, so the door was our only escape route. Ivan reacted to the presence of fresh snow by mixing it with milk powder to make ice cream. It was edible but not quite up to the standards of *Estonia*'s cuisine.

August was a cold month. There were some fine days for surveying, but to survive them I had to pile on so many clothes that I looked like Humpty Dumpty. Starting from the feet up, I wore moccasins with two thicknesses of sheepskin socks and two pairs of ski socks inside. From the waist down I wore windproof cotton trousers and inside them, leather trousers, duck-down trousers and wool underwear. My torso was protected by wool underwear, a Shetland pullover, an American quilted waistcoat, an Icelandic sweater, and a Russian down coat. On top of all that came an American lined anorak with a wolverine fur ruff and finally, a Russian anorak. On my head was a Russian sheepskin-lined leather helmet. Compromising between dexterity and freezing, I wore fur-lined, leather finger gloves inside a pair of truncated Russian dogskin mittens. With this outfit I could keep going for two to three hours before my feet became numb and I had to retreat to a warm hut.

Our rooms in the geophysics hut were not always warm. One day the temperature dropped to 14°C, although both heating elements were running and the tampion was blocking the ventilator hole. Mojmír had donned a beret to cover his shaven head, so I offered a round of port wine to warm the inner man. Quaffing his portion with relish, he exclaimed, *'Ach, zentrale heizung!'* 'Golden words,' added Tolya.

In spite of the cold, on 12 August I was able to report that my farthest stake, 12 km out on the ice shelf, was moving at the rate of 97 metres per year. I was learning what I wanted to learn about the deformation as the ice sheet flowed off the land and onto the sea. That evening I spoke with Kornilov at Molodezhnaya, comparing my results from Novolazarevskaya with our earlier work on Hayes Glacier. By this time I felt quite at home conversing on the radio in Russian, in spite of the attendant atmospherics.

Our nightly film shows over the winter included not only Russian films but also a few Albanian, American, Chinese, Czechoslovak, Danish, Egyptian, French, German, Hungarian, Italian, Polish and Romanian productions. Altogether we had 220 full-length feature films. The Soviet films were mostly made by 'Lenfilm' or 'Mosfilm' with an occasional 'Armenfilm'. Most of the foreign films had a perfectly synchronized sound track in Russian, so one would be virtually unaware that it was not originally Russian. We also enjoyed a couple of newsreels every night—newsreels never grow old. Some were of general Soviet news, some sport, and some edited from foreign newsreels.

The winter night sharpens the sense of humour, or perhaps the need for a laugh. ... Whenever somebody on the screen bears the remotest resemblance to one of us, a voice will pipe up from the audience saying who, the more incongruous the better. If a particularly haggard old man appears, it is 'Boriskin after a winter at Novolazarevskaya' or some such. These sallies are inevitably followed by wild guffaws...

Out for a walk one day, Nikolay and I clambered down to the foot of the rock cliffs rising sheer out of the sea. There we found a frozen lake at sea level. Though we did not know it at the time, the lake had been used for tidal measurements 18 months earlier. In spite of the conspicuous tide cracks along the shoreline, my assertion that there must be sea tides here was met with scepticism. The fact that my col-

106

leagues could not deduce it for themselves, I felt, was 'an amazing example of ultra-specialization in textbook technology'. Nikolay, however, agreed to collaborate in building a sea-level gauge to record over at least one full lunar month. Perhaps, I mused, we could also go fishing.

In due course Nikolay and Vasily, by dint of sheer hard work, hacked a hole through the three-metre thick lake ice to install our home-made tide gauge, built from a simple chart recorder. First, they had to line the hole with a piece of tubing before pouring down sufficient diesel oil to force the water out of the bottom. Only in this way could we ensure that it would not freeze. By making a sounding through the hole we discovered that the lake was 40 metres deep and, although tidal, was of fresh water from top to bottom. I call it a sea lake because on the seaward side it was surrounded by the floating ice shelf, and on the landward side by a rocky shore.

After some unsuccessful attempts, we built a frame to support the tide gauge. A weighted wire cable was then led over a pulley and through the hole to a heavier weight on the seabed. Now the rise and fall of the lake ice, and with it the tide gauge, was recorded on the chart. Over the next few months we obtained superb records showing a twice-daily oscillation with a spring tide range of up to 2.4 metres, and also unexplained short-period waves of smaller amplitude (seiches).[2]

In a run of good weather in early September, I was able to do more survey work than I had done in the previous three months. So much for winter surveying, I thought. However, it was an advantage to have spread the measurements over such a long period because it helped to check my calculations of the rate of ice movement. It was also one way to keep fit; carrying what I needed each day meant humping a 24-kilogramme rucksack back and forth.

I was not the only outdoorsman. Come fair weather or foul, Arkasha had to dress up and go out every six hours to read his meteorological instruments. Short and wiry, he always had time for a friendly wave if he caught sight of me on the causeway. Originally aiming to become a sculptor, he had studied at art school before changing tack and deciding to learn meteorology and oceanography at Leningrad Arctic College. Altogether he had worked on six different Arctic stations. Like so many of his colleagues, prior to coming here he had spent four years at the Druzhnaya station in Franz Josef Land. While based at Rudolf Island in 1958, he had straddled the Arctic Ocean by air, landing with a skiplane at 15 places on pack ice to make depth soundings and to lower temperature, salinity and current recorders. We celebrated his 27th birthday on 22 September. His

The tide gauge

Arkady (Arkasha) Maksimov

father was a blacksmith, which perhaps explained why Arkasha was at heart an artist and a craftsman. In his spare time during the winter, he fashioned an exquisite polar bear from walrus ivory, then mounted it on an iceberg carved out of perspex.

While Arkasha dealt with weather and solar radiation observations from the ground, the aeorologists Robert and Seva studied the weather far above the ground. Once every day, and sometimes twice, they launched a series of instruments attached to a hydrogen-filled balloon. It was easy on a calm day but in a blizzard it could be a struggle and, at these times, Arkasha was called in to help. Sometimes the balloon was torn from their hands and its precious instruments smashed on the rocks.

Once the balloon was launched, Robert rushed into his laboratory to check whether the radiosonde transmitter was sending its readings to his recording instruments, and Seva ran into a separate hut to track the balloon's progress with a radio theodolite. It could take hours for the balloon to reach the altitude at which it burst. One day in July the instruments reported an air temperature of $-87°C$ at an altitude of 20 km. All the observations were encoded and transmitted to Mirny daily.

Robert, I learned, was an only son who lost his father in the siege of Stalingrad. After five years in the Leningrad Arctic College he had

Seva with his radio theodolite

Robert reading meteorological instruments

111

wintered at Wrangel Island and also at the North Pole-7 drifting station. He had spent the winter of 1961 at Novolazarevskaya, immediately following the building of the station, so now he was enjoying his second winter at this spot. Married with one son, at home in Leningrad he worked at the Arctic and Antarctic Research Institute. He said that, although most of his colleagues lived in Leningrad, applications to work on the Soviet Antarctic Expedition came from all corners of the Union. Only a small proportion of aspiring *Polyarniks* were accepted. For his part, he said his motivation was not money but the chance to visit foreign ports.

Seva sported a pair of bushy black eyebrows and, unlike the others, kept a stubbly black beard. He was born and brought up in Belgorod, a town north of Kharkov on the border between Ukraine and Russia. After schooling there, he had trained as a radio engineer at the Leningrad Higher Marine Engineering School. During the International Geophysical Year in 1957–58, he had wintered at Druzhnaya station in Franz Josef Land. At the time, he told me, it had a complement of 60, one third of them women. Nearly all the women were employees in their own right, while at the same time being wives of men at the station. Seva's father died in 1946, but his mother was still a working doctor. Unmarried, he had a girlfriend working as a radio engineer at one of the Arctic research stations.

In late September, Vadim was laid low with a gastric ulcer. It was painful and Vasily felt that he should be evacuated to Mirny, where there were two doctors and better operating facilities. So Nikolay, Aleksey and I set off up the slope of the inland ice to look for an area level and smooth enough to land an aircraft. Driving a 25-tonne Tyagach for three people seemed like overkill, but I was told that the tractor needed exercise.

Proceeding due south, we passed a satisfactory bare-ice area and then a good snow area. However, Semochkin seemed bent on exploration, and pressed on towards a nunatak 20 km away. Seeing that he was heading for a slope with conspicuous snow-bridged crevasses, I suggested that we had come far enough. 'No, those are not crevasses,' I was told. Shortly afterwards the tractor lurched; Liosha yelled *Treshchina!* (crevasse) and stepped on the accelerator. We stopped and walked back to find a three-metre collapse under one track and a smaller one under the other.

Shaken, we stood shivering in the cold wind wondering what to do. I had brought a pair of skis and now put them on, preferring not to cross snow bridges while sitting on 25 tonnes of steel. I suggested that Liosha should turn the vehicle round and cross the crevasse at high speed, which he did. Some way back there was another black hole that we had opened on the way up. After I thought it safe to climb aboard, we followed our tracks back home.

This little adventure opened my eyes to the contrasts between life at Novolazarevskaya and my experiences in earlier years. We had set off up the hill with no food, no tent, no sleeping bags, no radio, no rope and no skis apart from my own. This lapse, and with it the inability to recognize crevasses, could have led to disaster. My colleagues, I now understood, were trained only to work in an observatory, whereas my work had required learning how to travel safely in unexplored country.

As the days wore on, Ivan found it more difficult to prepare attractive meals because some of his supplies were running low. On occasions the main course at dinner consisted of boiled potatoes—only boiled potatoes. As Ivan placed his big platter on the table, there were delighted cries of 'Wow! Boiled potatoes, *vkusniy* (delicious).' The potatoes were good and the enthusiasm was real. I feigned rapture and concealed my disappointment at having nothing more.

In October, there was a general election in Britain and at lunch Ivan asked what I thought of it. I said that I could not venture an opinion without hearing what the parties had to say for themselves. Ivan commented to the others, 'He's like the gypsies; as long as there's a horse market once a week, he doesn't care what government is in power.'

Once a month Ivan doled out our chocolate ration of 500 grammes. It took me only a few days to finish mine, but I wondered why I never saw the others eating theirs. One day, however, I found Pavel carefully packing his ration in an empty cigarette tin to take home to his family. Such is true love, I thought—and such the price of chocolate at home.

In contrast with dining on *Estonia*, here at Novolazarevskaya we had been using paper napkins at meals. However, like many things in Russia, they eventually ran out. As a substitute, we were given pages torn from the works of Lenin. Pretending to be shocked, I said, 'So this is all you think of the works of Lenin?' Quick as a flash, Tolya replied, 'Ah, but you see we know them by heart, so there is no longer any need to keep them.' But he could not hide the twinkle in his eye.

Another day Tolya heard on the radio that Christine Keeler, the British courtesan, had said in court that Mr John Profumo, the Secretary of State for War, had paid for her services. But she had not accepted money from another of her clients, the Soviet Naval Attaché, because 'he gave her greater pleasure.' 'Clearly,' said Tolya, 'Soviet men are the best in the world!' This was spoken in jest, but it

113

adhered to the politically correct myth that 'liberation of the working classes' under socialism would inexorably breed a superior race. Though in his heart Tolya never believed this, I admired his quick wit.

6 October. Fine and almost calm, $-20°C$. The days are really getting long now. If only we could have calm days a bit more often.

8 October. The Il-14 finally buzzed over and landed at the snow strip. ... Passengers Senko, Gusarov [doctor], Minkov and [Leontyev, a hydrologist]. We gave them a big welcoming party. ... One of the [crew] made a speech, after each sentence of which he squirted a CO_2 fire extinguisher over the table. ... Senko calmly picked a small bit of dry ice and put it in his tea, which was too hot to drink.

9 October. Up at 4 a.m. to go on an ice recco flight. ... The Il-14 is the one with an air force wing with a big red star. Apparently the 8th expedition [1962–64] collapsed the nose gear and ended up leaning on a crumpled wing. The only spare wing that could be found was in a military aircraft scrap dump. ... buzzed the station twice for me to photograph it.

We flew north, crossing a wide shore lead before encountering complete ice cover to latitude 63°S, where we turned round. At that point lunch was served: hamburgers, soup, bread, butter and coffee. There was a 'Glorious view of the main mountain range as we returned'. We landed after seven hours in the air.

The visitors left at 0500 the following day, taking Vadim with them to be kept at Mirny for observation. They also took 44 of our films, having exchanged them for 40 from Molodezhnaya. This meant that we could now show films every day of the week. With Vadim gone, our complement was reduced to 13.

9

Penguins and Petrels

Listening to the BBC news early on 16 October, I heard that Khrushchev had been deposed and his son-in-law had been removed as Editor of *Izvestiya*. On reporting this to my colleagues, they accepted the news calmly and at once began speculating on what might have led to the palace revolution. The next unsettling piece of news was that China had exploded its first atomic bomb.

The following day I caught sight of about 200 snow petrels wheeling and diving above the cliffs—the first birds of the season. Later we saw skuas and Wilson's petrels, and Liosha said he had seen three Adélie penguins approaching the station.

A week after Khrushchev was deposed, his portrait disappeared from the dining-room. He had become a non-person. From now on there was simply an unfaded patch on the wall where he had been. I later found his portrait in the clothing store, preserved, I guessed, in case he should ever be rehabilitated.

Throughout the winter I had detected no sign of 'cabin fever' among my colleagues. As a physiologist, however, Vasily had noticed a drop in blood pressure during the dark period and an increase of 5–10 beats/min in our heart rate. He sensed that we were more easily irritated. The first time I became aware of any problem was when Nikolay called a meeting to discuss a minor incident, in which Gherman and Arkasha nearly came to blows over whether or not the dining-room exhaust fan should be kept running during a film show.

In all my earlier Antarctic experience, such an incident would simply have been ignored by the others. But here it was different. We had gathered for a 'criticism and self-criticism' meeting in which all of us were to take part. We were seated in chairs placed against the walls of the hut on either side of the dining-table. After briefly describing the incident without apportioning blame, Nikolay asked the two men involved if either of them would now apologize for the fracas. However, each felt that the other was to blame. So clockwise round the room, the rest of us were asked in turn which of the men we felt was more to blame. The votes were about equal. Coming back to the combatants, they were asked if they wished to change their plea. They did not. So round the table we went for the second time. This time a slight majority felt that Gherman was more to blame. When his turn came, after a long pause, he apologized. Though to my mind the procedure made a mountain out of a molehill, it was democratic and it did clear the air.

Asked about this afterwards in private, Vasily said, 'Yes, but it can be misused.' He told how a similar procedure was used in the show trials of the 1930s. Guilty or not, the accused was required, sooner or later, to plead guilty. If necessary, torture was used to encourage the plea. Only then could the trial be brought to a close. I was impressed that Vasily, our senior Communist Party member, had no illusions about how justice was meted out during Stalin's reign. Few Russians did.

On 5 November, I brought out the port to celebrate Guy Fawkes day. Vasily asked whether we celebrated because the man tried to blow up parliament, or because he failed.

We were up at 0630 the following morning to hear the monthly expedition broadcast from Moscow. Slowly and clearly an announcer read a message from my wife. Everyone's letters reported that the family was healthy and all was well at home. My diary added: '...however much trouble they are having.' We knew that unpleasant news was often left out. Sadly, that served to devalue the genuine parts of the message.

Through my theodolite telescope I saw and then heard the plaintive squawking of an Adélie penguin a mile away, so I replied with my best imitation of a penguin squawk. After seconds taken by the sound to travel, I saw him suddenly raise his head with a jerk of astonishment at hearing another voice. Exchanging frequent calls, he waddled towards me for half an hour, stopping 50 metres off when he became suspicious of my squawks. Tracks through the station made it clear that penguins had visited during the night.

November 7th was the 47th anniversary of the 'Great October Socialist Revolution', the biggest of the year's three major feast days. We assembled outside for a *demonstratsiya*, with a flag-raising ceremony in which a large Soviet flag was flanked by the Czech flag and a red ensign—the only available British flag. For lunch, in addition to the food, we consumed three litres of cognac and two litres of champagne. Everyone except me had telegrams from friends and relations at home. However, I did receive one from George Meyer, the new US exchange scientist at Mirny. He had mail for me but lacked the means to deliver it.

October Revolution 'demonstration'

For some time, preparations had been made for a trip to the coast to bring fuel that was left behind in March. As before, I asked to go along in order to make measurements along the way. Five of us set out on 11 November in three artillery tractors. Liosha, Nikolay and Yura drove, while Vasily and I rode as passengers. To determine altitudes along the way, I had suspended a mercury barometer on an elastic cord from the roof of the cab. I also had a barograph suspended on elastic and cushioned with pillows.

Yura stopped at every stake along the trail for me to read the barometer, while he measured the stake. Trailing behind the others, we caught up with them on the summit of the coastal ice rise where they had stopped for the night. Inland, the whole mountain panorama was spread out before us. There was a splendid southern sunset, after which standing-wave cirrus clouds shone golden-red in the afterglow.

Moving on the next day, we found that our former landing stage had calved off on an iceberg, leaving only a 20-metre-high sheer cliff. However, the principal object of the journey was to pump 46 tonnes of fuel into four 14,000-litre tanks mounted on sledges. While this was going on, Nikolay and I walked along the ice wall to find a new landing stage to use when *Ob* came to pick us up. We found a seven-metre-high stretch of ice cliff that was ideal. Climbing down a snowdrift onto fast ice and crossing a tide crack, we walked further west before encountering a large crabeater seal asleep beside his access hole to the sea.

I had carried the barometer to sea level and back, so we could now calculate the height of our camp. On our return to the vehicles at 2000 just in time for the radio contact, conditions were bad and it was impossible to hear Gherman at Novolazarevskaya. On bringing out the morse key, it turned out that I was the only man present who knew the morse code. Nobody had been taught how to tune the radio, nor how to retune it to a different frequency. Luckily the morse codes for much of the Russian alphabet are the same as in English, and the radio operator Chernov had taught me the uniquely Russian symbols, so I did get our message across, albeit in pathetically slow time.

One of the 20-tonne sledges left by *Ob* a year ago had become frozen to the snow and could not be moved. Liosha put several sticks of dynamite under one runner and lit a length of quarry fuse. We retreated some distance before a colossal explosion shattered the runner and tossed heavy shards of steel high into the air. Many pieces fell among us. Glancing round first to check that nobody was injured, our little group collapsed in fits of laughter. Escapades like this, dangerous though they were, did much to weld us into a team. The sledge, however, was now unusable.

Homeward-bound the next day, each sledge together with its load weighed 35 tonnes. Liosha's vehicle had wider tracks than ours and he forged ahead to the top of the hill. Meanwhile, Nikolay stripped some teeth from his first gear and failed to move his load. Hitching up in tandem with Yura, we still failed to move the double load. So Liosha came back and pulled us up the hill one at a time. From the top Nikolay forged ahead, but Yura and I still could not move without help. Liosha backed up his sledge and hitched us together in tandem. Together we were now hauling 70 tonnes and, including the weight of the tractors, the whole train weighed 120 tonnes. It was a formidable display of sheer power.

We camped after 38 km on reaching the first icy patch, hoping that the absence of snow would make it easier to move off in the morning. Nikolay's vehicle had opened three small crevasses, but they were not of a size to cause concern. I found that the mileage measured by vehicles pulling in tandem was 15 per cent greater than the actual distance travelled. This meant that in their struggle to keep us moving, the tracks were slipping by that amount. I had noted earlier that, driving with no sledge, the mileometer accurately measured distances.

Starting off in the morning, each of us became bogged down in soft snow and had to be rescued. Seeing our struggle from afar, Pavel and Robert drove out from the station in a GAZ, and helped many times to hitch and unhitch the loads. We finally reached home in a straggling line to be welcomed with hugging and hand-shaking as though we were long-lost cousins. I always found these uninhibited welcomes heart-warming; it was a display of emotions that would be unheard of on any British expedition. At the station, the bathroom was already heated up and we sat down to a 'wet' supper followed, in my case, by ten hours of deep sleep.

November 17th was my 38th birthday and it was celebrated in style.

I was presented with one of 15 volumes of Stendhal, each member of the station having one other on his birthday, Treshnikov's book of the history of Antarctica, a complete radiosonde, an amber tiepin and some souvenirs of Leningrad. Tolya even sacrificed some chocolate. Nikolay and Vasily made speeches in Russian and so did I. Tolya and Seva made speeches in English.

21 November. We heard today for the first time that we are to be relieved last, not first, therefore probably in March rather than in December. All are glad.

The following day eight of us went on a grand *ekskursiya*, starting out in two GAZ machines. However, after one of them broke down, we jumped on the other and continued westwards over a series of ice-covered lakes off the northern shore of our long nunatak. After bumping along for 10 km, we found ourselves driving over a two-kilometre-wide lake. The lake was said to be 100 metres deep and to have once lost its ice cover in a particularly warm summer. At that time a flying boat could have landed on it, and it was more than wide enough to surface any submarine that chose to come here under the ice shelf from the open sea.

In the middle of the lake was an island, and on it we came across nine Adélie penguins, including four pairs nesting and one sitting on an egg. Later we found three more penguins, one of them sitting on two eggs. We were amazed to think that every one of these birds must have waddled across the ice shelf from its seaward face some 75 km away to the north. There would have been no food along the way, no food where they were nesting and no food on their way back.

Adélies nest only on rock. Vassfjellet is so low-lying that it cannot be seen from the ice front, so how did they know it was here? We wondered whether their species could have retained some atavistic

Yura with nesting Adélie penguin

memory from the time, perhaps thousands of years earlier, when the ice shelf had not yet formed. Or might they have smelled the rock from the open sea, or at least smelled the mosses and lichens that grow on it? In a sense, of course, they were nesting by the sea, or at least by a freshwater lake that was connected beneath the ice shelf with the sea. While it is conceivable that there were fish or krill in the lake, we thought it unlikely. We even discussed whether penguins could swim under the ice shelf, perhaps finding air pockets to breathe along the way. However, having seen some of them waddling towards Vassfjellet from the north, we discounted that as unlikely.

Further west we came upon a spectacular wasteland of icebergs dying, or so it seemed, under the onslaught of intense summer melting. But they were being forced together by pressure from the north and must have been bonded by regelation. Some were right against the shore and had pushed ridges of boulders and beach debris to a height of seven metres. Our cameras clicked wildly as we made a record of this wonderland of ice forms. The only water visible was right along the shoreline.

We returned home invigorated by the sight of so much dramatic scenery. I felt it was the most interesting five hours that I had spent

120

Aerial photograph of the western end of Vassfjellet. At the foot of the 100-metre-high cliff is a tidal sea lake. The ice shelf in the foreground is moving towards the shoreline and melting

since arriving at Novolazarevskaya. So much natural beauty and so many unsolved riddles.

Five days later Seva, Yura, Vasily and I set off on the longest *ekskursiya* of the season, to the extreme western end of the nunatak. While I carried a rucksack with food and spare clothing, the others brought nothing—no windproofs, no gloves and no food. Vasily wore a trilby, the others berets. As a cautious man, I could not help wondering what would happen if a storm blew up, but the weather gods were kind to us.

At our farthest west, a lake was separated from the inland ice by only a few metres of rock. Ice blocks had calved and slid into the lake from above. We were astonished to find what appeared to be the tracks of two dogs climbing a snow slope.

[The tracks] were somewhat weakened by evaporation, but unlikely to be penguin tracks since the individual fingers were visible, the spacing large, and there were no wing marks, even on a steep slope. In early 1961 two huskies, Laza and Rev, were brought to [Novolazarevskaya from the coast]. After a week they disappeared, and never returned.

It is possible that they could have survived on penguins and, after making their way to the ice front, perhaps also on seals. One mummified seal had been found near Novolazarevskaya by an earlier expedition.[1]

We walked back along the middle of our nunatak, tiring because of the rough boulders and slippery lichen. But there was unlimited clean water in lakes along the way to slake our thirst. Reaching home at 1800 with aching limbs, we sat down to a supper of boiled potatoes and tinned fish.

Soviet Constitution Day, 5 December, happily was also a 'wet' bath night. As a very special treat, the evening meal included fresh cucumber that Arkasha had grown in his window box. Later we enjoyed tomatoes from the window boxes in the dining-room.

There was another long *ekskursiya* on 9 December. Seven of us walked to the big sea lake and beyond. It was the hottest day yet, so

Summer relaxation by a sea lake

122

Iceberg scenery. Note man on the sea lake (left). This is the same area as shown in the aerial photograph on p. 121

some were stripped to the waist and paddled barefoot in the sea. I think the popularity of these excursions owed much to the joy and freedom that we all felt at the coming of summer.

On another day, I clambered down to the sea and cut a permanent bench mark on a slab of bedrock near sea level. Then I determined its height above mean sea level from the tidal records. Later, Robert and I made an optical levelling survey, finding that the height of the station barometer was 102 metres above mean sea level, not 87 as I had been told. Now poor Arkasha would have to add 1.5 millibars to his barometer readings to correct them to sea level.

I made another experiment to establish which of my stakes was on grounded ice and which afloat. This involved taking vertical angles to them from the nearest survey station at high-water springs (the time of which we had determined) and then again at low water. The stakes on grounded ice were not rising and falling, the others were. It was a simple and elegant solution and the results were conclusive.

The snow covering the slope from the east end of our nunatak to the tidal lake was by this time saturated with meltwater. Nobody witnessed what must have been a spectacular slush avalanche that stripped away last winter's snow along a one-kilometre path, scoured the previous summer's surface and filled its former melt-stream

123

A natural sub-surface stream supplying our domestic water

channels. The slush came to rest in three-metre-high ridges at the foot of the slope. The alarming thing was that the gentle 1 in 25 slope down which it careered was not one that we thought steep enough to be unstable, and I had often travelled over the area. Had anyone been on it at the time, the avalanche could have been lethal.

Closer to home, the small lake from which we drew domestic water was hit by a flash flood. The night before it happened, we could have walked across the ice. The next morning on my way to breakfast I beheld Pavel rowing a dory across it. The pumping-station was floating on its side and being rescued by the mechanics. The main station buildings were in danger of being flooded by the rising water level. Later in the day, dynamite had to be used to open a drainage channel along a snow-filled trench by the pigsty. Eventually our piped water supply was restored.

Nikolay's 33rd birthday was on 17 December and, by coincidence it was also the day on which, four years earlier, the first team of construction workers had arrived here to build Novolazarevskaya station. His father, a woodsman from a village east of Slobodskoy in the foothills of the Urals, was severely wounded in the war and now worked on a collective farm, as did his mother. Nikolay had trained as a merchant seaman at Leningrad Nautical College before moving to the Arctic and Antarctic Research Institute to take jobs in the

The pump house sinking in the summer flood

125

Arctic. He wintered at Dickson Island off the mouth of the Yenisey river, and later served on the North Pole-6 drifting station. While calibrating radiation instruments, he had visited almost all the Soviet Arctic stations.

As leader at Novolazarevskaya, he took his responsibilities seriously; indeed his lips seldom parted in jest. With me he was polite but invariably formal, still perhaps seeing me as representing an alien culture, whereas to the others I was just one of the gang. Whenever he addressed me in his official capacity, it would be: 'Charles, I have to inform you that...' or 'I am unable to reply to that question', rather like a diplomat charged with communication between governments.

At home he lived in Leningrad with his wife Alina and son Igor. Together they enjoyed a total living area of 40 square metres—twice as much as their statutory entitlement. Nikolay hoped to buy a Moskvich car with the proceeds of his Antarctic work.

In his office in the Pentagon, Nikolay kept a small lead chamber into which at different times he put precipitated dust, soil, lichen, moss, water, snow and ice. The object was to study their natural β-radioactivity. A detector within the chamber fed a counter outside. It seemed more of a hobby than a research programme, though it must also have been monitoring radioactive fallout from nuclear bomb

Nikolay Yeremin with his radioactivity apparatus

tests. Nikolay did have other hobbies: he was carving walrus tusks and building a Geiger counter.

One day I found him reading *The Bolsheviks*. While discussing politics I mentioned the name of Lavrenti Beria, the former head of the NKVD (secret police), who during Stalin's reign arranged for the 'disappearance' of millions of people on trumped-up charges. Most of those arrested were never seen again. Nikolay first went pale, then flushed with indignation and said that, if I ever mentioned that name again, 'Soviet people will be angry.' Beria had become a non-person—expunged from history. Indeed his name is nowhere to be found in the 1970 edition of the 30-volume *Bolshaya Sovetskaya Entsiklopediya* (Great Soviet Encyclopedia). Western sources, however, record that he was convicted of conspiracy in 1953 and shot.

Christmas Day was not celebrated, though there was a celebration because it was the anniversary of the Proclamation of Soviet Power in the Ukraine. It was also the day that our toilet paper supply ran out. Old copies of *Pravda* came in handy from then on.

On really calm days, Yura, Tolya and I sunbathed naked in the lee of the hut, sometimes for an hour at a time. On the warmest day in November (+5°C), we went for a swim in a pond, one side of which was dammed by an ice cliff. One minute in the water was about my limit. The slightest breeze would end such frolics and send us scurrying indoors for clothing.

On 31 December, we toasted the New Year with champagne at 2100 because that was midnight in Moscow. Three hours later we reconvened for toasts at midnight local time, by then imbibing home-brew. I took the opportunity to present diplomas to the graduates of my English class. With summer upon us, there was no longer any time for lessons. Nor for films, though we continued to have repeats of some favourites. I asked to see again *The Russian Miracle*, a four-hour-long East German historical documentary about the Soviet Union in the 20th century. Popular Western films included *Meet me in Las Vegas*, *The Egg and I*, *The Man with a Thousand Faces* and *Roman Holiday*

Nikolay set about making an inventory of everything that was to be handed over to the new crew. In the course of this he found a discrepancy between the quantities of liquor that he had issued and the amount remaining in the store. Altogether, 108 bottles of vodka, champagne, or eau-de-Cologne had vanished without trace, as well as quantities of tobacco.

A meeting was called to discuss the discrepancy. Seeking the guilty party, Nikolay stared at each of us in turn. Finally, head bowed, Ivan confessed that he had something to do with it. While everyone knew

A brief swim to cool off after hard labour

Sunbathing

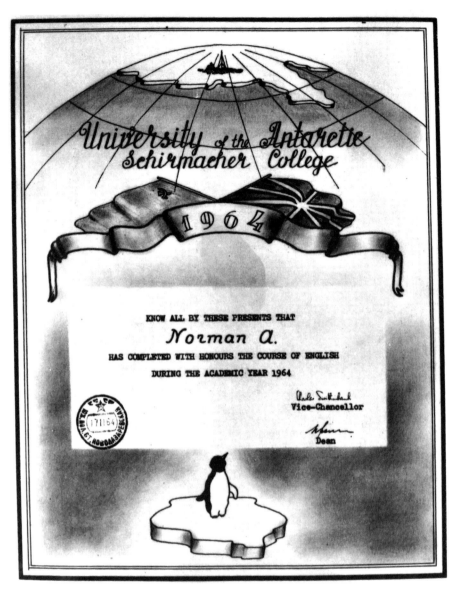

KNOW ALL BY THESE PRESENTS THAT

Norman A.

HAS COMPLETED WITH HONOURS THE COURSE OF ENGLISH

DURING THE ACADEMIC YEAR 1964

Vice-Chancellor

Dean

Graduation certificate for the author's English classes

that Ivan was in the habit of taking solo walks after dinner, we had assumed that it was to get a breath of fresh air as an antidote to the heat of the kitchen. Now, it transpired, his evening walks had masked other pastimes. Russians, I knew by now, enjoyed a drink or two.

However, I had underestimated their ingenuity when deprived of it. Eau-de-Cologne, it transpired, was an esteemed substitute when vodka was in short supply.

Throughout January and the first half of February, I continued my survey work, finally finishing on 15 February. On fine-weather days I would be out and about, while on bad-weather days I would compute the results. Finally, I wrote a full report for those who might continue the work in years to come. I wrote it in English but, when I had finished, Tolya kindly set about translating it. Meanwhile, I drafted all the maps and diagrams to go with it.

10

A Near Miss

Our isolation was now inexorably drawing to a close. *Ob* left Molodezhnaya on 18 February to head our way, and the following day Nikolay, Liosha, Yura and Vasily left for the coast driving three Tyagach machines with sledges and a caboose.

At the request of the oceanographer in *Ob*, Pavel, Arkasha and I drove down to the sea lake and moved the tide gauge to a new site that was less affected by melting. The oceanographer proposed to make simultaneous tidal measurements at the coast to see whether there was a phase difference between his tides and ours. I took the opportunity to suspend a fishing-line through the ice with meat and bread on a home-made hook. This provided much amusement for my sceptical colleagues, and I was tipped off about a plot to plant a tinned fish on the hook. But there was no fresh fish.

Our last days were spent frantically packing and tidying up the station to give a good impression to the newcomers. On 21 February *Ob* arrived at the coastal ice rise and began unloading cargo. The following day, we heard by radio that our tractor train had left the coast, towing not only all the general cargo for the next (10th) expedition but also bringing the relief crew for the coming winter. Driving almost non-stop, they reached Novolazarevskaya at 1630. Out jumped 14 new smiling faces to greet us. With them were two visitors, Yury Razumov, a film cameraman, and George Meyer, a microbiologist and friend from my days at the American McMurdo station. Meyer brought me a fat packet of mail from the ship and a few other letters sent from McMurdo.

That evening there was a festive party with all 29 of us spread before a lengthened table. There was much exchanging of news after which all retired in varying states of sobriety. Unfortunately I was duty boy, so had no sleep at all and spent half the night washing dishes.

I was relieved to discover that among the newcomers there were two glaciologists, both of whom were keen to carry on my work. One of them, Yury Kruchinin, was to be leader of the station for the 1965 winter. The other, Igor Simonov, had spent the winter of 1962 at Novolazarevskaya and was delighted to be back in familiar surroundings. Knowing the place as well as I did, Igor was able to take over not only the equipment but also all of my survey work without difficulty. I handed over a copy of the full report that I had drafted in English and Tolya had translated into Russian.

After sleeping off my exhaustion, I read letters from home late into the night. Some made depressing reading. Communicating in privacy for the first time, my wife felt able to tell me not only about what had gone well for the family in my absence, but also what had not gone well. Gallantly, she was weathering it all, while I, unable to lift a finger to help—except with words—felt desperately inadequate. I began counting the days.

Our team left Novolazarevskaya for the last time on 26 February in company with four of the newcomers. At the coast we loaded our gear on *Ob*, said our farewells, and steamed out into the mist.

The next day Yury Razumov handed me a brand new Zenith camera that Vadim, convalescing at Mirny, had asked him to give me to mark our friendship during the winter. The voyage eastward along the coast gave us an opportunity to wind down after the frantic efforts to tidy up and finish our work at Novolazarevskaya. It was relaxing to find that now, in contrast with last year's voyage, I could converse fluently in Russian with anyone on board. Somehow they too were more relaxed because I was accepted as a full member of the expedition, of belonging to that close-knit fraternity that characterizes all who have lived and worked in Antarctica. One man said that I spoke Russian like a peasant, by which I think he meant that I spoke it ungrammatically. Tongue-in-cheek, I replied, 'Surely in a worker's paradise, all of us should be speaking like peasants.'

My colleagues were busy editing and polishing reports of their work to hand in when they reached home. I had access to them all but most were too technical for my level of understanding. I asked Arkasha to show me what his report said about the year's weather at Novolazarevskaya. He said that September 1964 was the coldest month ever, with an average temperature of −20.5°C. The mean annual temperature had been −10.8°C, and the mean annual wind speed 16 knots.

I read Yura's report of his aurora studies. He said that there had been 57 nights with aurora out of 143 clear nights during the year. His film record was 980 metres in length and was to be analysed in Leningrad.

Besides report-writing, I found my colleagues playing tennis. Now totally empty, the forward hold had a vast bilge deck on which a full-sized tennis court had been laid out, complete with whitewash markings and net. For those less ambitious, there was table-tennis.

We arrived at Molodezhnaya on 4 March and, during a five-hour stay, brought on board many homeward-bound friends and acquaintances from last year's voyage. They included Dmitry Maksutov, the expedition's chief engineer, who had made my first few days on *Estonia* easier than they might have been because he spoke English.

From here on I offered half an hour of English conversation daily at 0800 for anyone interested. George Meyer helped and we generally had a dozen or more students, including on occasion the Captain.

It had been difficult to find English texts ... that sustained their interest, until George Meyer brought on board a copy of John Cleland's *Memoirs of a Woman of Pleasure*. The pupils not only became diligent but enthusiastic, there was a waiting list to read it, and bedside lamps were on at all times of the night to snatch a few extra pages. The book seems to deal with situations that have universal appeal...

One day an event occurred that might, at a stroke, have destroyed my faith in the integrity of the Soviet Antarctic Expedition, or at least some members of it. One of the cabin stewardesses had been told to clean out the laboratory on the boat deck where I had been making a fair copy of my diary and field notes. Both the originals and the fair copies had been put in a drawer to keep the place tidy. Doing what she was told, the stewardess had emptied all the drawers into a waste bin and was about to heave the contents over the side, when Arkasha walked in. Recognizing the nature of her 'rubbish', he stopped her just in time.

What upset me immeasurably was the realization that, if she had disposed of everything that I had recorded in the last 15 months, I would never have believed that it was due to a misunderstanding. Instead, I would have concluded that it was an official act to deprive me of my records, while explaining this away as an accident. Such was the mind-set of the Cold War in 1965. Now, 37 years after the event, I still bless Arkasha for his presence of mind.

Along the coast of Enderby Land, at one point there were 800 icebergs on the radar screen within 25 km of the ship. No wonder Captain Sviridov slowed down or stopped at night. It would take a collision with only the tiniest 'growler', a small piece calved from an iceberg and awash, to hole a ship.

We anchored off Mirny on 14 March. I spent a day ashore and

noted how much better the food was than ours at Novolazarevskaya. The whole Aviation Division came aboard, together with all 1964 winterers who had not already left on *Estonia*. One of the homebound doctors told me that during the course of the year he and his colleagues had performed 14 surgical operations, 11 of them appendectomies. I wondered whether the Antarctic environment raised the incidence of appendicitis or whether it was simply that the doctors felt a need to keep their hand in.

George Meyer, who was to stay at Mirny, gave me letters and specimens to take home for despatch to the US National Science Foundation in Washington. *Ob* put to sea after much waving, blasts on the siren and rockets from both ship and shore. Our era had ended and an eager new team had taken over the reins.

This time we were headed not for Fremantle but for a very long voyage to Abidjan, on the Ivory Coast of west Africa, to load 500 tonnes of redwood for a Danish furniture company. It was nothing to do with our expedition, but Soviet economics dictated that no ship should return empty from any part of the world if there was a cargo to be carried. Since *Ob* and every other ship was government-owned, we had no choice.

18 March. Still pitching in a following sea. Food consists of a small number of standard dishes endlessly repeated: cutlets, macaroni and minced gristle, goulash, meaning rice with stewed gristle, pork chop, rice with fried gristle, potato with chipped gristle. Also compote twice daily, which is just coloured stewing water.

20 March. Pitching heavily in a force 8 head sea. My copies of *Time* magazine [four months old] are eagerly culled from cover to cover, being forbidden in USSR. They quickly disappear from the music room where I put them, and later I see them in use in someone's cabin.

I visited the crew's mess-deck, finding it tidy and reasonably comfortable. But instead of the scantily-clad women that would adorn the bulkheads of an American ship, there were long red banners painted with slogans such as: 'Brotherly greetings to all nations struggling for peace, democracy and socialism' and 'Long live the peaceful Leninist foreign policy of the Soviet Union'. Before the evening film show, there was a half-hour lecture by the First Mate on recent 'news'. We were informed of Soviet successes, American aggression in south-east Asia, negroes rioting in Alabama and Chinese students wounding policemen in Moscow.

Maksutov gave a fascinating lecture on the development of the Soviet merchant fleet since the 1917 revolution. The ultimate ambition of the Northern Sea Route (northeast passage), he said, is for Soviet ships to take over all the far east trade of the whole of northern Europe by carrying cargo more cheaply the short way.

Party meetings were held in the lounge every few days. I listed some of the sermons:

The character of our age and the general lines of the peaceful communist movement.

The struggle for peace and the development of the peaceful revolutionary process.

The world socialist system—the decisive contemporary revolutionary factor.

Marx-Leninism on the law-governed building of socialism and communism.

The international significance of the building of communism in the USSR and its influence on the development of the peaceful revolutionary process.

Marx-Leninist teaching on the role of the masses and the role of individuals in the historical process.

The development of the programme of the Communist Party of the Soviet Union on Marx-Leninist teaching in the Soviet state.

The present stage of the struggle of the working classes in capitalist countries.

The present stage of national freedom movements.

No wonder I was not the only one who found them soporific. I treasure a photograph that Razumov took of me as I slept soundly through one of the sermons.

30 March: After lunch sunbathed for an hour. ... Yet another film about life on a collective farm, with everybody singing as usual. I have seen a good many films with bad plots, but never so many with no plot at all.

It was 5 April, three weeks after we left Mirny, before *Ob* crossed the Equator. By then there was an open-air swimming pool, films were shown on deck and, owing to a lack of ventilation in the cabins, at night every hatch was covered with bedding and men sleeping under the stars. Worst off were the engineers: the air temperature in

Swimming pool on *Ob*

Ob's only 'air-conditioned' accommodation

their main control room rose to 52°C. Polar ships, I was learning, are ill-equipped for the tropics

The following morning I was invited for drinks with Mikhail Ostrekin, the expedition leader, and found Nikolay and the Captain already quaffing a bottle of wine. After half an hour of small talk, Ostrekin said that he had received word that I could stay in the ship all the way to Leningrad. Some weeks earlier I had sought permission to do this. The news was considered sufficient cause for a celebration, so the First Mate (and ship's commissar) Viktor Tkachev was summoned together with another four bottles of wine and half a bottle of cognac. These, of course, did not leave the table until they were empty. Inevitably, I spent the afternoon on my bunk recovering.

Two days into the northern hemisphere, we steamed into the lagoon at Abidjan and immediately began loading giant 10–15 tonne logs from barges bringing them alongside. I was given permission to go ashore, but my colleagues were held back to wait for an agent carrying local currency.

By African standards, Abidjan looked prosperous, and I noted that people of every colour were riding in taxis, of which there were many. The Chargé d'affaires at the British Embassy handed me mail from home that had been sent by diplomatic bag, then directed me to the British Information Centre, where Mr William Abbott agreed to send home a parcel of microfilms of all my records. I still had not recovered from the near-loss of the original notebooks, and here was good insurance.

Another day dawned with only a fraction of the logs loaded. Somebody arranged for a bus to go sightseeing, so the next morning 28 of us set off with no guide apart from a French-speaking driver who asked me where he was to take us. I suggested a representative selection of what the country had to offer. So he took us to a National Park followed by the Abidjan zoo.

> Then to a very crowded native bazaar, the first for most people. The ability to communicate without knowing the language is not one the Russians possess, and they get rather lost in trying to buy anything, do not haggle and so get robbed.

My colleagues seemed subdued. Tolya explained that they had been told to be wary of *provokatsiya*. Asked what that meant, he explained that enemies of the USSR sometimes provoke Russians abroad, causing a 'diplomatic incident'. Since there were no diplomatic relations between Moscow and the Ivory Coast, all hell could break loose. I assured him that they were safe in my hands, whereupon the driver took us to the Presidential Palace. This was closed to the public, but our driver, believing that we were Americans, asked the palace guard if we could have a tour of the building. Knowing that our chances might be better as Americans, I did not disillusion him. All formalities were swept aside, and we were led into the palace past armed guards with fixed bayonets. Unaccustomed to such deference, my colleagues were nervous, but I told them to bask in their temporary status as Americans. Playing their part, they took out their cameras and flashed in every direction.

The palace was in tropical modern style with the most lavish interior furnishings—red plush carpets, oak panelling, marble portals and exquisite mosaics. Asked to sign the visitors book on behalf of the group, I entered 'British' in the nationality column. It was, after all, part of the truth.

Outside, we found a small but expectant crowd, so we joined it. To our delight and astonishment, three magnificently-clad potentates appeared out of a door and were driven away in an open limousine with a motorcycle escort preceded by a police car with siren wailing. We waved, applauded and photographed them. Afterwards I learned that we had applauded the President of Côte d'Ivoire, Félix Houphouët-Boigny; the President of Niger, Hamani Diori; and the President of Togo, Nicolas Grunitzky. They were off to the airport to meet President Yaméogo of Haute-Volta, who was returning from a visit to the US on board President Lyndon Johnson's 'Air Force One'. My colleagues wondered if I had contrived to lay on the whole show for them.

Loading of the redwood logs was finished the next day. From the bridge of *Ob* there was unmistakeable evidence that the Ivory Coast's overseas trade was booming. Through my binoculars I saw ships from Britain, Denmark, France, Greece, Holland, Japan, Norway, Panama, Sweden, Switzerland, West Germany and Yugoslavia. Most were loading redwood but also some coffee and copra.

Rigorously obeying the troika rule, my friends went ashore in threes. Several asked me to help them with shopping. High on their list of priorities were erotica, contraceptives, sleeping-pills, patent medicines and, for those who could read English, detective stories, all these being unobtainable at home. They bought clothing for themselves and for their wives, and spare parts for their cars. Vasily wanted an ignition switch to make his Volga harder to steal. One brave soul bought three books that were banned at home: Ian Fleming's *From Russia with Love*, Aldous Huxley's *Brave New World*, and George Orwell's *Nineteen Eighty Four*. I took some comfort from the fact that my English classes at Novolazarevskaya seemed to have broadened their cultural outlook.

I was the only one who sent letters home. My colleagues did not dare to mail anything without permission, and permission was not forthcoming. It was unlikely that they even risked asking for it.

Late in the day we cast off and put to sea. The crew and the expedition members were each presented with two large oranges and two thin slices of pineapple. At the next meal we even had some long-life milk, flown, we were told, from Paris. All the ship's fresh provisions, however, were exhausted after a week, and we went back to the old diet.

Over the next few days, high seas accentuated the boredom felt by most of us, and Party meetings did nothing to alleviate it. Daily eulogies of Lenin were broadcast over the ship's loudspeaker system, and I sat through Maxim Gorky's reminiscences of him. Not many people were actually listening, having been subjected to the same thing since childhood. Nikolay spent a week writing a sermon on Lenin to be read on Lenin's birthday.

News came through that 13 new cars were to be made available for distribution among the 132 returning members of the expedition. This reflected the fact that, in the Soviet Union, there was a waiting list for cars. Not only did one need money but also a place on the waiting list. Thirteen of us were to be allowed to jump the queue as a reward for Antarctic service. As more than 13 wanted to buy cars and had the money, a lottery was arranged. The winners were ecstatic; the losers would have a second chance after another winter in the Antarctic. In preparation for the excitement of car ownership, there was a twice-weekly gathering to discuss the highway code. Aspiring drivers played endlessly with toy cars, buses, trams, pedestrians and policemen meeting at crossroads or overtaking.

Steaming through the English Channel, I suffered pangs of homesickness from thinking how near yet how far I still was from home. I caused considerable mirth by resorting to bottle post. Into each of five empty champagne bottles I put a letter to my wife, international postal reply coupons, and three Russian cigarettes as a reward to the finder. I learned later that, miraculously, two of the letters reached home before I did. Evidently one of the senders had tried the cigarettes, and had written on the envelope: 'You did the right thing with those cigarettes—threw them in the sea!' I knew what he meant; I too had discovered that our Russian cigarettes were, to put it mildly, an acquired taste.

In the Baltic on 28 April we had to plough through some thin pack ice. Entering the canal at Leningrad, *Ob* passed the icebreakers *Sibiryakov*, *Moskva* and *Kapitan Belousov*, before making fast next to the cruise ship *Baltika*. We were met by a large crowd, a band playing and much speech-making. My colleagues had to cope with immigration and customs papers, but I was left alone. Each returning hero was greeted on the quay with hugs and kisses from his family.

Tolya took me by taxi to the *Oktyabrskaya* hotel. Asking for my passport, the lady at the front desk began thumbing though its pages looking for the Soviet visa. Becoming frantic as she reached the last page without finding anything, she looked at me in horror and demanded an explanation. Tolya told her that I had permission to be in the country but there had been no opportunity even to stamp my passport.

As soon as I got into my room I phoned home; it was the first time I had spoken with my wife in 17 months. For the next eight days I was generously and exhaustingly entertained by the staff of the Arctic and Antarctic Research Institute and by my colleagues. By chance, my visit coincided with an official visit by Valter Schytt, the Swedish glaciologist with whom I had worked in the Antarctic 15 years earlier. Valter had come by car with his wife, driving through Finland. Together we did a lot of sightseeing and visiting. One of the highlights of our stay was the May Day parade. Tens of thousands of citizens took part or watched from the pavements, and so did we. After the leaders and major trade union delegations had filed past with their colourful banners down Nevsky Prospekt, the main street, we joined the parade and marched with it all the way to Palace Square and past saluting stands where civil and military dignitaries took the salute. The general public, we noted, were free to join or leave the parade at any point and, except when we were passing the saluting stands— eyes left—the atmosphere was festive and delightfully informal.

Summoned to the Institute by its director, Aleksey Treshnikov, I found myself asked to describe my work at Novolazarevskaya before an audience of about 80 people. Unprepared, I managed to speak without notes for half an hour, after which Treshnikov stood up and thanked me not only for my work but for my success in presenting it 'in clear and understandable Russian'. Treshnikov's words made my day.

Treshnikov explained that the total cost of the Soviet Antarctic Expedition was about 3.5 million roubles (£1.4 million) per annum. However, that represented only one fifth of the total output of the institute, the rest being concerned with the Arctic.

There followed presentations of books, a tour of the institute, a tour of the Hermitage Museum, and an exquisite performance of 'Swan Lake' at the Kirov ballet. In the interval we were led to the bar and consumed a glass of champagne poured over a bowl of ice cream, something I had not tried before; it was delicious.

141

With heavy luggage because of everything I had brought from the Antarctic, now supplemented by generous gifts of books (including a four-volume set of the works of Alexander Pushkin), I decided to leave Leningrad by taking a train to Helsinki. Mischievously, and knowing that it would cause consternation, I went to the ticket counter at the station and, using my best Russian, asked for a single ticket to Helsinki. The pretty girl behind the counter looked horrified and spluttered '*Nelzya!*' (It is forbidden, as indeed it was at the time). Furthering my provocation I asked, 'Why not? I have money.' Now angry, she demanded: '*Pass!*' I handed her my British passport, at which point she breathed deeply, recovered her composure, and informed me that only Intourist could issue a ticket. This I knew, but I had enjoyed the harmless *provokatsiya*.

I left Leningrad on 7 May. Tolya, Robert, Arkasha, Yura and Seva came to see me off at the station, and also Leonid Balakshin, Communist Party Secretary at the institute. I noticed that Balakshin stood apart from my colleagues, showing that he had come to say farewell in his official capacity. For me it was a sad parting. With the Cold War as it was, I doubted whether I should ever see these wonderful people again.

At the Finnish border my baggage was minutely searched by two polite but thorough KGB men. They flicked through many of my books looking, I suppose, for letters that I might be carrying on behalf of friends to Russian émigrés. Then they asked for my wallet and disappeared with it along the corridor. This concerned me as I had names and addresses in there that I preferred them not to follow up. After a couple of minutes I wandered casually along the corridor and found the two men discussing the contents of my wallet. I politely asked for its return and it was handed to me.

On arriving in Helsinki, the contrast could not have been greater. For me there was a feeling of sudden release as if a great weight had been lifted from me. No officials asked for papers nor cared who I was. Henceforth, I could travel wherever and whenever I wanted, without asking anyone's permission. I was back in the Western world.

At home in Cambridge five days later, I had much to tell but much more to ask.

EPILOGUE

At home I tried to compensate for the high-carbohydrate diet of the previous 18 months by consuming high-protein foods like meat, fish and cheese. This made me ill and I was unable to hold down any food. On summoning a doctor and explaining the circumstances, the prescient practitioner at once diagnosed 'prisoner-of-war syndrome'. He knew that, on being liberated, prisoners of war had demanded high-protein foods and suffered the same fate. The solution was simply to wean me slowly from the Russian diet.

My Antarctic comrades had become friends for life. At home, however, we were all once again pawns in the Cold War. Though I could write freely to them, their messages became stilted and formal. Indeed, they did not write letters but sent only New Year cards with a printed greeting and best wishes for continuing good health. That way they felt safe from the censors. But I knew that such formalities would not diminish our friendship.

I had spent a wonderful and fulfilling 18 months with a small group of warm-hearted and accomplished people; indeed the most congenial community I had ever lived with in the Antarctic. Their cultural background had been fascinating and revealing. I respected them and admired their easy-going acceptance of the discipline of their masters. Occasionally we had discussed politics, but nobody ever set out to convert me and it would have been easy to keep off the subject.

Yet paradoxically, 1964 was the most stressful year I have ever spent in the Antarctic. Why? It was quite simply because of the mental isolation from most of the basic tenets with which I had been brought up, and the concurrent immersion in an alien faith. None of my comrades was in any way to blame, and of course none of them suffered from the same sense of isolation. But so great was the pressure that I realised why, in the long run, people in similar circumstances sometimes capitulate. Fighting a long and lonely battle within oneself could lead to a mental breakdown. I began to understand how total immersion in any religious tradition—and I see communism as one—can overwhelm the mind. Throughout history, surely, that has been their strength.

Had I come any closer to understanding the triumphs and evils of the Soviet system? I felt that I had. Although as an ideology, communism seemed to have much in common with Christianity, one of its fundamental tenets was that, sooner or later, the state would wither away and material goods would be distributed equally. Yet in Soviet practice (to paraphrase George Orwell) some were more equal than others. Perhaps the ideals of Marx-Leninism can, or could be, approached in a monastery. They require that men, like monks, should voluntarily sacrifice their inherent self-interest and their wish, as individuals, to have control of their own lives. At least for the majority, that sacrifice will always go against the grain. I concluded that in the long run, communism, like Soviet socialism, could never prevail over democracy.

At Novolazarevskaya, we dealt with life as we found it. Ideology was irrelevant. My colleagues and I responded in the same way to any given set of circumstances. It is ironic that, in the Soviet Union, we would think and act differently. Guided by ideology, our responses would not be the same.

My impression of all the Russians with whom I worked was that they had a high standard of technical education leading to greater specialization than in the West. This in turn led to some lack of adaptability. A high level of specialization is only possible on a large polar expedition in which all the necessary specialists can be found. In my own experience on earlier expeditions, much of our work consisted of operating with a party of three or four men perhaps hundreds of kilometres from anyone else. I have at one and the same time had to serve as leader, glaciologist, navigator, radio operator, driver, mechanic and surveyor. Another interesting contrast was that only a small proportion of the staff of the Soviet expedition expected to analyse and publish their own results. Most of them simply handed in their data in Leningrad for analysis by someone else. In our little group there was only one exception: Vasily wrote a book on his physiological work.[1]

Evidently in part owing to centralized planning, the strongest characteristic of the Soviet scientific programme was the carefully standardized collection of data in a number of established fields. There was less probing of new fields.

I was disappointed that the results of my work at Novolazarevskaya were circumscribed by travel restrictions. However, I had accurately determined the position of the grounding line and also the rate of deformation of the ice sheet at many points within 13 kilometres of

144

the station. These findings were considered of such interest that they were extended by others when travel subsequently became possible. Later my report became part of a larger published study, with generous acknowledgement of my contribution.[2] My snow accumulation and ablation studies were included in another paper.[3] In addition, I published two general accounts,[4,5] and wrote a 91-page illustrated report giving technical details of the Soviet stations and their research work.[6]

Garik Grikurov, the Russian geologist who had been the other half of my exchange, thoroughly enjoyed his 18 months with the British Antarctic Survey. In October 1965, I was invited to lecture about my experiences before the Royal Geographical Society in London. Afterwards Sir Vivian Fuchs, Director of the British Antarctic Survey, spoke:

> I wonder whether our friend Grikurov is speaking today in the Soviet Union about his experiences with the British, and if so, will he be putting across quite so good a picture? I hope and believe he would. We found him an extremely companionable and intelligent man, besides being very hard working and having a great sense of humour. Certainly we could not have had a better representative from that country...[7]

The good feelings engendered by the exchange benefited both sides. Grikurov himself held a strong enough position in the Institute of Arctic Geology in Leningrad to correspond directly with me and other members of the British Antarctic Survey on matters of mutual interest. As far as collaboration was concerned, we had overcome the barriers. Nothing has changed since.

One example will suffice. Eighteen years later, in 1983, in pursuing the work of my team, I wrote to Grikurov asking whether the Soviet expedition would consider carrying in their ship 100 drums of BAS aircraft fuel from Halley, one of our stations, to Druzhnaya II, a Soviet station 850 kilometres to the west. This would provide a fuel depot for our aircraft and save our ship from a time-consuming diversion from her planned itinerary. BAS offered to pay the Soviets for their services. Grikurov replied:

> Our ships will try to collect 100 drums at Halley. ... If for some reason loading operations at Halley appear impossible, your aircraft can always refuel from our stock at either of Druzhnaya bases. ... This, of course, will not involve any financial obligations on your side—we can easily spare 100 drums.[8]

All this at a time when the best-known Russian word in the West was *Nyet*. Sceptical as some of my British colleagues had been in 1963 about the value of an exchange of scientists with the Russians, they now accepted that it had proved worthwhile.

Thirty years passed before I was able to meet my Russian comrades again. We arranged to have a reunion in St Petersburg over the Easter weekend in 1995. My wife was invited but no other wives came. Two of our number could not be traced, five had died, but the surviving seven were all present (Gherman Floridov, Seva Ladygin, Arkasha Maksimov, Robert Pyzhov, Pavel Tsvetkov and Nikolay Yeremin). It was a poignant and emotional occasion and many a tear was shed as we bear-hugged each other in the way that Russians do. Our friendship was undimmed and reminiscences flooded back.

None of my Soviet colleagues had an apartment large enough to hold a big dinner party, so Oleg Zhukov, the doctor from Molodezhnaya, kindly invited us to his place high up in a tower block. We feasted, we drank a lot, we proposed toasts galore, and we made speeches in Russian and speeches in English until the early hours.

Some of their stories of the last 30 years were harrowing. Nikolay apologized for not having written a proper letter since we parted in 1965, explaining that he had been involved in secret research on radioactivity and could not have risked being suspect. He had also served on drifting stations in the Arctic Ocean from which British and American nuclear submarines were tracked on their voyages under the ice. For my part I revealed that, unbeknown to him at the time, I myself had been in one of those submarines.[9]

Arkasha, who had served in oceanographic research ships, told me that he had several times visited British seaports. I said, 'Why on earth didn't you come to visit or at least telephone me?' By way of explanation he drew a finger sharply across his throat and added 'KGB!'

As I finish writing this account in the year 2001, Nikolay and I are corresponding by e-mail. He kindly sent me his own account of our expedition, written for the benefit of his family.[10] Many things in Russia have changed since 1965, but all too many have not.

APPENDIX

It took five years

Throughout the Cold War from 1946 until the break-up of the Soviet Union in 1991, Antarctica remained a haven of peace in a troubled world. It still is today. Eighteen nations maintain year-round research stations on the continent, and there is collaboration between them.

An international forum known as the 'Scientific Committee on Antarctic Research (SCAR) has coordinated Antarctic science since 1958.[1] At its meeting in Moscow in that year, SCAR agreed to 'encourage the interchange of field geologists and glaciologists working in different regions of the continent'. This set me thinking. What if I was to propose an exchange of scientists between Britain and the USSR—and then apply to fill the post?

My reasons for wanting to join the Soviet Antarctic Expedition were twofold. As a glaciologist, I had spent five years studying the movement and deformation of Antarctic glaciers. I knew that the Russians had built a station exactly at the boundary between a floating ice shelf and the grounded ice sheet, and I knew that this critical transition had never been studied.

I also wanted to learn Russian, and isolating myself with Russians seemed the easiest way to do it. However, if I failed to make a go of it, there would be no escape. In common with most other Antarctic expeditions at the time, once a ship put a man ashore, he would remain there for 12 months—come what may. For a number of years I had rubbed shoulders with foreigners but the same could not be said of the Russians. To them I would be a curiosity, under suspicion that I had been sent by my government to see what they were up to.

None of that concerned me. I was at the time unmarried and carefree, and nobody had put me up to it. But there was no precedent in Britain for an exchange of scientists of this nature, so there would be many a hurdle to jump before I could head south.

In December 1958, I began by asking Dr Gordon Robin, Director of the Scott Polar Research Institute in Cambridge, to make a proposal to the 'British National Committee on Antarctic Research'

147

convened by the Royal Society. At the time I was on the staff of the Institute and engaged in a study of the distribution of pack ice in the Northwest Passage on behalf of the Government of Canada.

Three months later I wrote to Professor G.A. Avsyuk and Professor P.A. Shumsky, two leading Soviet glaciologists with whom I was on friendly terms after meeting them at scientific conferences. Both responded favourably and suggested that either the Royal Society or the Scott Polar Research Institute should approach the Soviet Academy of Sciences in Moscow on my behalf.

Gordon Robin asked Dr David Martin, then Executive Secretary of the Royal Society, to open discussions with the Russians. However, the bureaucratic obstacles were many. Britain's permanent Antarctic expedition, the Falkland Islands Dependencies Survey (FIDS),[2] had no interest in an exchange of scientists. Even if we could persuade FIDS, the Russians would still need to find one of their scientists willing to complete the exchange.

I wrote to Academician Shcherbakov of the Soviet Academy of Sciences; to Professor V.V. Frolov, Director of the Arctic and Antarctic Institute in Leningrad; to Mr A.A. Afanasyev, the Chairman of Glavsevmorput[3] (the organization responsible for the logistical support of Soviet Antarctic expeditions); and to Professor M.M. Somov, the leader of those expeditions. They were surprised and a little baffled at receiving an application from an individual. Such things did not happen in their country.

At the same time I tried another tack by asking the Royal Society to approach the British Council, which had just reached an agreement on cultural exchanges between the UK and the USSR. This they did but nothing came of it.

During the Cold War it took rare courage for any Russian to correspond with someone in a foreign country, unless officially authorized to do so. In a land where individual initiatives were frowned upon, the only accepted channel of international communication was upwards through the Russian scientific hierarchy to the top, thence from one national academy of sciences to the other (in our case the Royal Society), and finally downwards through our own hierarchy.

To compound the difficulties, in those days it sometimes took months to get a reply from anyone in the USSR owing to their vestigial fear—inherited from Stalinist days—of the consequences of stepping out of line. The safest course for any individual was to reply *nyet* to foreign nitiatives. Moreover, many letters arriving in Moscow from abroad were censored, as were outgoing letters. Sometimes there was simply no response. When an answer did reach me from the

148

Academy of Sciences in May 1959, it simply stated that they had no vacancies for glaciologists.

That was a setback because I was due to finish my Arctic sea-ice research at the end of September and, with it, my contract with the Scott Polar Research Institute.

My work there had given me a fascinating excursion into the history of the Northwest Passage. In the space of four years I had travelled roughly 100,000 kilometres to collect data on the distribution of pack ice in Arctic Canada. The scientific results appeared in the form of a most unwieldy atlas.[4] Years later I wrote about this work in *Forty Years on Ice*.[5]

Now I needed to find employment. Luckily I had received offers from three American universities and from the Australian government, so it was a matter of selection depending—as far as I was concerned—on how interesting the work promised to be. All of them offered field work in the Arctic or the Antarctic, which was what I wanted.

Finally, and still without progress on the Russian exchange, I accepted a post as Research Associate at the University of Michigan in Ann Arbor, USA. This was in response to an invitation from Professor James H. Zumberge, a geologist who had worked in the Antarctic. The University of Michigan had a long tradition of polar research and I could count on support there.

Meanwhile, intergovernmental discussions were continuing about the need for a general agreement on the management of Antarctic affairs. After many months, these culminated in the drafting of a treaty. The Antarctic Treaty, as it is known, was signed in December 1959 by the 12 nations working in the Antarctic at the time.[6]

The need for a treaty arose from a common interest in preventing the militarization of Antarctica, and to accommodate differing views on sovereignty. Seven of the signatory states claimed sovereignty over sectors of Antarctica, and the British, Argentine and Chilean sectors overlapped. None of the claims was recognized by the United States or the Soviet Union. Reconciling these differences was a brilliant feat of diplomacy, and the treaty laid the groundwork for cooperation that has stood the test of time.

The Treaty guarantees free access to the continent for any peaceful purpose. Article III states that in order to promote international co-operation in scientific investigation of Antarctica 'to the greatest extent feasible and practicable ... scientific personnel shall be exchanged in Antarctica between expeditions and stations.'

So here was another string to my bow. However, now I would have to pursue my ambitions from the other side of the Atlantic.

I spent 2½ very happy years at the University of Michigan, during which time I led three Antarctic expeditions, married a lovely Alaskan, acquired a stepdaughter and added another daughter. Later I wrote about those expeditions in *An Alien in Antarctica*,[7] so in this account I have skipped over that period of my life.

While in the US, my ambition to take part in an exchange with the Russians was undiminished. In mid-1961 I asked Gordon Robin to reopen the question. By that time, Gordon was Secretary of SCAR and therefore in a strong position to make a direct approach to the Soviet Academy of Sciences. The reply from Moscow was unhelpful, suggesting that as I was living in the US, I should approach the US National Academy of Sciences with a view to representing the American side of a US/USSR exchange.

Not to be deterred, Gordon again asked the Royal Society to pursue the matter. This they did, and one by one the obstacles that had seemed insuperable began to fall away. Sir Vivian Fuchs, Director of FIDS, would accept a Russian at a British base provided that he was a good scientist. A reasonable enough stipulation, I thought, but the inference that he might not be must be kept from the Russians.

Another difficulty, as far as I was concerned, was to find an employer who was prepared to do without me for 18 months—while at the same time paying a salary into my bank account. As sole breadwinner in a family of four, this had now become essential. In due course Sir Vivian Fuchs agreed that, if an exchange could be arranged, FIDS would sponsor a post for me at the SPRI. The salary would be half the size of my American salary, but I was in no position to quibble. As a quid pro quo for arranging this, Gordon Robin asked that, on returning from the Antarctic, I would join the staff of the Institute. To this I agreed.

Time passed and, in February 1962, seven months after the Royal Society had reopened negotiations with the Soviet Academy of Sciences, the Russians accepted an exchange 'in principle' but would not say *when* I could go south. After three years of negotiations, the uncertainty was galling. Some months later, the Royal Society yet again tackled the Russians. At the same time, as an act of faith, I resigned from my post at the University of Michigan and, together with my family, moved back to Cambridge.

A favourable response came from Moscow on 22 August 1963. Now I had just three months in which to prepare for an absence of 18 months. It had been a long haul. I would be leaving my wife and our two children to fend for themselves, and we were expecting a third child. Not even in the direst emergency could I get home from the Antarctic. The thought would give pause to any family man. But my wife had known of my plans for years and had always encouraged them.

150

NOTES

Prologue

1. I have avoided formal transliteration of Russian names in the text to make them easier to read in English.
2. James Cook, *A voyage towards the South Pole and round the world performed in His Majesty's ships the Resolution and Adventure, in the years 1772, 1773, 1774, and 1775*, 2 vols. (London, Strahan and Cadell, 1777).
3. Thaddeus Thaddevich Bellingshausen, *The Voyage of Captain Bellingshausen to the Antarctic Seas*, edited by F. Debenham, 2 vols. (London, Hakluyt Society, 1945).
4. Soviet expeditions are numbered consecutively beginning with their first winter in the Antarctic in 1956. Thus we were the ninth.

Chapter 1

1. Charles Swithinbank, *Foothold on Antarctica. The first international expedition (1949–1952) through the eyes of its youngest member* (Lewes, The Book Guild, 1999).
2. Charles Swithinbank, *An alien in Antarctica. Reflections upon forty years of exploration and research on the frozen continent* (Blacksburg, Virginia, McDonald and Woodward, 1997).
3. These are gross registered tons of 100 cubic feet measured according to nautical conventions. Throughout the book I quote speeds in knots; distances, heights and weights are given in metric units.
4. Christopher Pala, 'Unlikely heroes: The story of the first men who stood at the North Pole', *Polar Record*, 35:195 (1999), pp. 337–342.
5. Apsley Cherry-Garrard, *The worst journey in the world*, 2 vols. (London, Constable, 1922).
6. P.A. Shumskii, *Principles of Structural Glaciology. The petrography of fresh-water ice as a method of glaciological investigation* (New York, Dover publications, 1964).

7. All times of day in this book are in hours and minutes according to maritime practice; thus 0619 is 6:19 a.m. and 1805 is 6:05 p.m.
8. The word *tovarishch* means comrade. I use the word interchangeably with colleague, having been assured that, in Russian, the use of *tovarishch* does not necessarily have political overtones.
9. Forty years on, however, we still do not know whether ice sheets are ever actually in equilibrium with climate.

Chapter 2

1. Committee for State Security, the Soviet secret police.
2. *Ob* was of 130 metres overall length, 19 metres breadth, 7500 gross registered tons, 4250 net registered tons, and 12,600 tonnes displacement at maximum draft. The hold grain-capacity was 10,500 cubic metres. Four eight-cylinder diesel engines, built in the Netherlands from German designs, were coupled to British-built generators. These in turn fed a 7000-horsepower, British-built electric motor driving a single shaft.

Chapter 3

1. A.V. Nudelman, *Soviet Antarctic Expeditions 1959–1961* (Washington DC, National Science Foundation, 1962), pp. 24–25.

Chapter 4

1. *Artilleriiskiy Tyagach Tyazheliy*, a heavy artillery tractor.
2. Indented quotations are from the author's diaries.
3. Sir Douglas Mawson, *The home of the blizzard*, 2 vols. (London, William Heinemann, 1915).
4. Amphibious tracked army vehicle designed for landing on shores and traversing snow-covered terrain.
5. Aviation gasoline in 200-litre drums.

Chapter 5

1. Andrey Kapitsa was born in England while his father, the physicist Peter Kapitsa, was working at the Cavendish Laboratory of the University of Cambridge.

2. Summer in the Antarctic extends from November to February, thus from one calendar year to the next.
3. Charles Swithinbank, *Foothold on Antarctica. The first international expedition (1949–1952) through the eyes of its youngest member* (Lewes, The Book Guild, 1999).
4. Alfred Ritscher, *Wissenschaftliche und fliegerische Ergebnisse der Deutschen Antarktischen Expedition 1938/39*, 2 vols (Leipzig, Koehler & Amelang, 1942).

Chapter 6

1. *German* is the Russian form of the German name *Herman*. It is spelled with a G in this work because the letter H corresponds with *X* in Russian. In English I have added an h (Gherman) in order to indicate pronunciation with a hard G, unlike the soft G in German.
2. Charles Swithinbank, *Foothold on Antarctica* (Lewes, The Book Guild, 1999), pp. 188–90.
3. L.I. Rogozov, 'Self operation', *Soviet Antarctic Expedition Information Bulletin*, 4:4 (No. 37), pp. 223–24 (Washington DC, American Geophysical Union, 1962).

Chapter 7

1. The wind-chill factor was developed by Paul A. Siple and Charles F. Passel in 'Measurements of dry atmospheric cooling in subfreezing temperatures', *Proceedings of the American Philosophical Society*, 89:1 (1945), pp. 177–99. A more recent version of windchill is by W.G. Rees, 'A new wind-chill nomogram', *Polar Record*, 29:170 (1993), pp. 229–34.
2. Charles Swithinbank, 'Ice movement in the McMurdo Sound area of Antarctica', *International Association of Scientific Hydrology*, Publication No. 86 (1970), pp. 472–87.

Chapter 8

1. *Nimbus 1* was launched from California on 28 August 1964, two days before I saw it.
2. I hold most of the original records. The Harmonic Constants were determined in June 1966 by G.W. Lennon of the Liverpool

Observatory and Tidal Institute (now Institute of Coastal Oceanography and Tides). The seiche records were analysed by V.F. Zakharov, 'Seiches in the vicinity of Novolazarevskaya station', *Soviet Antarctic Expedition Information Bulletin*, 6:3 (No. 60), pp. 268–69 (Washington DC, American Geophysical Union, 1967).

Chapter 9

1. Vladimir Bardin, 'Discovery of seal mummies in the Schirmacher Ponds', *Soviet Antarctic Expedition Information Bulletin*, 1:4 (No. 31), 1962, p. 28.

Epilogue

1. V.V. Boriskin, *Zhizn' cheloveka v Arktike i Antarktike* (Leningrad, Meditsina, 1973).
2. Yu.A. Kruchinin and I.M. Simonov, 'Izucheniye lednikovoy tektoniki i morfologii lednikov v rayone stantsii Novolazarevskoy (Antarktida), *Izvestiya Vsesoyuznogo Geograficheskogo Obshchestva*, 100:3 (1968), pp. 212–22.
3. Yu.A. Kruchinin, 'Inversiya Glyatsiologicheskoy zonalnosti v vostochnoy chasti berega printsessy Astrid', *Trudy Sovetskoy Antarkticheskoy Ekspeditsii*, 38 (1968), pp. 61–76.
4. Charles Swithinbank, 'Russians in Antarctica', *Geographical Magazine*, 38:10 (1966), pp. 748–61.
5. Charles Swithinbank, 'A year with the Russians in Antarctica', *Geographical Journal*, 132:4 (1966), pp. 463–75.
6. Charles Swithinbank, 'Technical notes on the ninth Soviet Antarctic Expedition 1963–65' (1965, unpublished).
7. *Geographical Journal*, 132:4 (1966), p. 475.
8. Letter of 29 August 1983 from Grikurov to Swithinbank.
9. Charles Swithinbank, *Forty years on ice* (Lewes, The Book Guild, 1998), pp. 61–78.
10. *Pyteshestvye k ledyanomy kontinenty* (Voyage to the ice-covered continent). Unpublished.

Appendix

1. Before it was renamed in 1962, SCAR was known as the 'Special Committee on Antarctic Research'.
2. Renamed the British Antarctic Survey from 1 January 1962.
3. Glavnoe Upravlenie Severnogo Morskogo Puti (the Chief Administration of the Northern Sea Route).
4. Charles Swithinbank, *Ice Atlas of Arctic Canada*. Ottawa, The Queen's Printer, 1960.
5. Charles Swithinbank, *Forty Years on Ice*, Lewes, The Book Guild, 1998 (pp. 5–19).
6. Argentina, Australia, Belgium, Chile, France, Japan, New Zealand, Norway, South Africa, UK, USA and USSR. Over the ensuing 40 years, a further 31 states have acceded to it.
7. Charles Swithinbank, *An Alien in Antarctica*, Blacksburg, Virginia, McDonald & Woodward, 1997.

GLOSSARY

Ablation	All processes by which snow, ice, or water in any form are lost from a glacier.
Aerology	A branch of meteorology dealing with the air.
Anorak	A windproof outer garment.
Antarctica	The Antarctic continent and its surrounding islands within the continental shelf.
Blizzard	A storm of drifting snow.
Caboose	A shelter mounted on a sledge or tractor. The equivalent term in American is wanigan.
Calving	The breaking-away of a mass of ice from a floating ice shelf, glacier, or iceberg.
Crevasse	A fissure formed in a glacier, ice sheet, or ice shelf. Crevasses are often hidden by snow bridges.
Deadmen	Buried logs used in mooring a ship to ice.
Depot	Supplies left in the field for later use.
Earth currents	Natural electrical currents flowing in the crust of the Earth and induced by currents flowing in the ionosphere.
Fast ice	Sea ice attached to the shore or to an ice shelf. An abbreviation of landfast ice.
FIDS	Falkland Islands Dependencies Survey (British Antarctic Survey from 1962).
Floe	A piece of floating ice other than fast ice or glacier ice.
Geomagnetic pole	The end of the axis of the geomagnetic field which surrounds the earth and extends into space.
Geomagnetism	Terrestrial magnetism.
Geophysics	The physics of the earth including the fields of seismology, volcanology, magnetism and geodesy.
GLAVSEVMORPUT	Chief Administration of the Northern Sea Route.

157

Grounding line	The junction between a floating ice shelf and an ice sheet resting on rock.
Growler	A small piece calved from an iceberg, and often awash.
Hypothermia	Cooling of the body to danger level as a result of heat loss from exposure.
Iceberg	Large mass of floating or stranded ice which has broken away from a glacier or ice shelf.
Icefoot	A narrow fringe of ice attached to the coast, unmoved by tides and remaining after the fast ice has broken free.
Ice front	The vertical cliff forming the seaward face of an ice shelf or other floating glacier, varying in height from 2 to 50 metres above sea level.
Ice rise	A mass of ice resting on rock and surrounded either by an ice shelf, or partly by an ice shelf and partly by sea. No rock is exposed and there may be none above sea level. Ice rises generally have a dome-shaped surface. Large ice rises may have dimensions of 100 kilometres or more.
Ice rumples	Locally grounded areas overridden by moving ice. Ice rumples occur within or at the seaward margin of ice shelves.
Ice sheet	A mass of ice and snow of considerable thickness and large area. Ice sheets may be resting on rock (inland ice sheet) or floating (ice shelf).
Ice shelf	A floating ice sheet of considerable thickness attached to a coast. Ice shelves are usually of great horizontal extent and have a level or gently undulating surface. They are nourished by the accumulation of snow and often by the seaward extension of land glaciers. Limited areas may be aground.
Ice stream	Part of an ice sheet in which the ice flows more rapidly and not necessarily in the same direction as the surrounding ice. The margins are sometimes clearly marked by a change in direction of the surface slope, but may be indistinct.
Ice wall	An ice cliff forming the seaward margin of an inland ice sheet or ice rise.
Inland ice sheet	An ice sheet of considerable thickness and more than about 50,000 square kilometres in area, resting on rock. Inland ice sheets near sea level may merge into ice shelves.

Ionosphere	Part of the outer fringe region of the atmosphere containing free electrically charged particles.
Knot	A unit of speed equal to one nautical mile per hour.
Komsomol	The Young Communist League.
Kulak	A landowning farmer employing labour.
Krill	A small crustacean *Euphausia superba*.
Lead	A navigable passage through floating ice.
Mirage	Optical phenomenon in which distant objects appear uplifted above the horizon. Caused by abnormal refraction with a surface temperature inversion—in which air temperature increases with height.
Moraine	Ridges or deposits of rock debris transported by a glacier. Common forms are: lateral moraine (along the sides), medial moraine (down the centre).
Nunatak	A rocky crag or small mountain projecting from and surrounded by a glacier or ice sheet.
Pack ice	An area of sea ice other than fast ice, no matter what form it takes or how it is disposed.
Polyarnik	Anyone who makes a career of working in the polar regions.
Radiosonde	Meteorological sensors attached to a balloon. Instrument readings are transmitted to the ground by radio.
Radio theodolite	A directional aerial used to track radiosonde balloons.
Regelation	Fusion of two ice bodies, generally under pressure.
Sastrugi	Sharp, irregular ridges formed on a snow surface by wind erosion and deposition. The ridges are parallel with the direction of the prevailing wind.
Sea ice	Any form of ice found at sea which originated from the freezing of sea water.
Seismograph	An instrument for automatic recording of earthquakes or artificial explosions.
Serac	A sharp ridge or pinnacle of ice on a glacier or icefall.
Snow bridge	An arch formed by snow which has drifted across a crevasse, forming first a cornice, and ultimately a covering which may obscure the opening.
Snowdrift	An accumulation of wind-blown snow deposited in the lee of obstructions or heaped by wind eddies.
Sovkhoz	A State farm.

159

Sputnik	Man-made Earth satellite.
SPRI	Scott Polar Research Institute.
Tabular	The most common type of iceberg in Antarctic waters, flat-topped and generally calved from an ice shelf.
Theodolite	A precise angle-measuring instrument consisting of a telescopic sight mounted on graduated horizontal and vertical circles. Fixed to a stable tripod, a theodolite is capable of measuring the angle between any two points sighted through the telescope to one millionth of a 360-degree circle. Geodetic theodolites are even more accurate.
Tyagach	A heavy artillery tractor.
UNESCO	United Nations Educational Scientific and Cultural Organization.
USSR	Union of Soviet Socialist Republics.
Weasel	Amphibious tracked snow-vehicle.
Whiteout	A condition in which daylight is diffused by multiple reflection between a snow surface and overcast sky. Contrasts vanish and the observer is unable to distinguish snow surface features.

INDEX

162